ELSE LASKER-SCHÜLER

THE BROKEN WORLD

ANGLICA GERMANICA SERIES 2

Editors LEONARD FORSTER, S. S. PRAWER *and* A. T. HATTO

Other books in the series

ELSE LASKER-SCHÜLER

THE BROKEN WORLD

HANS W. COHN

CAMBRIDGE UNIVERSITY PRESS

Published by the Syndics of the Cambridge University Press
Bentley House, 200 Euston Road, London NW1 2DB
American Branch: 32 East 57th Street, New York, N.Y.10022

© Cambridge University Press 1974

Library of Congress Catalogue Card Number: 73-80481

ISBN: 0 521 20292 2

First published 1974

Printed in Great Britain
at the University Printing House, Cambridge
(Brooke Crutchley, University Printer)

To Catherine

CONTENTS

CONTENTS

PREFATORY NOTE

The theme of this enquiry grew out of many talks with Catherine Küster-Ginsberg, a close friend of Else Lasker-Schüler. It was in these talks that the person and work of the poet became alive and meaningful to me, and in which there arose the questions which I try to answer. Without her, this book would not exist, and I am deeply grateful to her for helping it into life and watching its growth.

I also wish to express my thanks to Professor Elizabeth M. Wilkinson, of University College London, whose unfailing interest in the progress of this enquiry and whose innumerable suggestions offered constant help and support.

Quotations from the work of Else Lasker-Schüler are made with the permission of her literary executor, Mr Manfred Sturmann, Jerusalem, and of Kösel-Verlag, Munich.

H. W. C.

ABBREVIATIONS

GW Else Lasker-Schüler, *Gesammelte Werke* in drei Bänden, hrsg. von Friedhelm Kemp und Werner Kraft, Munich, 1959–61.
(The volume number is given in Roman, and the page number in Arabic numerals, e.g. GW, III, 10.)

BK Else Lasker-Schüler, *Briefe an Karl Kraus*, hrsg. von Astrid Gehlhoff-Claes, Cologne and Berlin, 1959.

DD Else Lasker-Schüler, *Dichtungen und Dokumente*, hrsg. von Ernst Ginsberg, Munich, 1951.

All quotations from Else Lasker-Schüler's work and letters are taken from these collections; the idiosyncratic spelling and punctuation are her own.

To distinguish between Else Lasker-Schüler's use of dots and my own indication of ellipsis, I have used the sign (. . .) to indicate passages omitted.

1. INTRODUCTION

When Else Lasker-Schüler's first collection of poetry, *Styx*, appeared in 1902, her friend and teacher, the vagabond-poet Peter Hille, wrote about her:

> Ihr Dichtgeist ist schwarzer Diamant, der in ihre Stirn schneidet und weh tut. Sehr wehe. Der schwarze Schwan Israels, eine Sappho, der die Welt entzweigegangen ist. (DD, p. 565)

These few sentences not only express the tragic nature of this poet's creative gift, they also indicate its roots: her 'world' has 'broken apart'. Hille's insight points to a way in which her work can be approached. This way might perhaps be formulated first as a question: what was this poet's 'world', and in what manner had it 'broken apart'?

It is my intention to attempt an answer to this question by examining Else Lasker-Schüler's poetry. One might expect to find a poet's mode of being revealed most tangibly in his work, and I have decided to limit my field of examination by concentrating on her poetry, drawing on her prose only in order to illuminate or elaborate the meaning of the poems. For I think we can agree with Werner Kraft 'daß diese Prosa künstlerisch nicht auf der Höhe der Lyrik steht'.[1] Her prose writings (and this includes also her two published plays) have often something of the nature of lyrical exercises and contain the essence of her poetry in a more diffuse way. They sometimes help to elucidate the poems, but they never achieve their concentrated impact. They do, however, contain many useful biographical references.

BIOGRAPHY AND CRITICISM

This raises the question of the part biography can play in such a study. Heinz Politzer[2] feels that it is unnecessary to know

[1] W. Kraft, *Else Lasker-Schüler* (Verschollene und Vergessene), Wiesbaden, 1951, p. 15.
[2] H. Politzer, 'The Blue Piano of Else Lasker-Schüler', *Commentary* IX, New York, 1950, p. 336.

anything about Else Lasker-Schüler's life in order to understand her poetry, and Sigrid Bauschinger[1] agrees with this. Such a view seems to me to separate the inseparable, to break up the organic unity which a poet and his work presents.

The poem can be seen as an act in which the poet realizes himself at one specific moment of his life, and the form which this realization takes will be an aspect of the poet's existence at this particular moment. This again is part of the poet's total 'history', if by this we understand both outer and inner happenings, and his reactions to them.

I am aware of entering controversial territory. Whether a writer's 'history' – in this wider sense – should be taken into account in an examination of his work has been a subject for discussion by English and American critics since the twenties. There developed a strong trend in what is called 'The New Criticism' to dissociate the poem from the poet and examine it as an 'object' in its own right. This was a welcome reaction against a tendency to put the emphasis on life, feelings and intentions of the poet while neglecting what he had written. The 'New Critics' rejected the substitution of biographical essay and psychological treatise for critical appreciation, and insisted on the importance of the text and its structural qualities.

Nobody held this view more emphatically than T. S. Eliot, who was also perhaps the first to formulate it when he wrote in 1919:

> Poetry is not a turning loose of emotions, but an escape from emotion: it is not an expression of personality, but an escape from personality.[2]

From this passionate avowal that the 'personality' of the poet had no bearing on the assessment of his poetry the way led to an increasing 'fixation upon the analogy between a poem and an object' which Walter J. Ong considers 'characteristic of the present English-speaking world'.[3] It led, for instance, to W. K.

---

[1] S. Bauschinger, *Die Symbolik des Mütterlichen im Werke Else Lasker-Schülers*, Diss., Frankfurt-Main, 1960, p. 20.

[2] T. S. Eliot, *Selected Essays*, London, 1934, p. 21.

[3] W. J. Ong, 'A Dialectic of Aural and Objective Correlatives', *Essays in Criticism*, London, 1958, p. 166.

Wimsatt's and M. C. Beardsley's indictment of what they call 'the Intentional Fallacy' which they describe as

> a confusion between the poem and its origins, a special case of what is known to philosophers as the Genetic Fallacy... It begins by trying to derive the standard of criticism from the psychological causes of the poem and ends in biography and relativism.[1]

René Wellek and Austin Warren, in their attempt to answer the question 'what and where is poetry?', also reject 'the view that the genuine poem is to be found in the intentions of the author'[2] and after repudiating the 'alternative suggestions – that the genuine poem is in the total experience, conscious and unconscious, during the time of creation',[3] they arrive at the definition of the work of art as

> A system of norms of ideal concepts which are inter-subjective. They must be assumed to exist in collective ideology, changing with it, accessible only through individual mental experiences based on the sound-structure of its sentence.[4]

This abstract formulation shows the care with which the personal element has been eliminated. The person of the reader or spectator is still granted some ghostlike survival in the form of 'individual mental experiences', but the author of the work of art himself no longer appears.

In suggesting a more personal approach to the examination of poetry, I do not propose a return to methods which use the writings of an author only in illustration of 'Life and Times'. The 'New Criticism' has established beyond doubt the importance of the text as centre and point of departure of a valid critical examination. But among the questions to be asked when studying the text these also seem to me legitimate, and even necessary: who is the person whom this work expresses, what are his specific experiences and how do they manifest themselves in what he has written? After attempting to answer such questions

---

[1] W. K. Wimsatt and M. C. Beardsley, *The Verbal Icon*, Yale University Press, 1960, p. 21.
[2] R. Wellek and A. Warren, *Theory of Literature*, London, 1949, p. 148.
[3] *Ibid.* p. 149.   [4] *Ibid.* p. 157.

from the text, it seems to me a desirable extension of the critical procedure to go to other sources, outside the work itself, for further illumination.

S. E. Hyman who defines modern criticism

> crudely and somewhat inaccurately as the organized use of non-literary techniques and bodies of knowledge to obtain insights into literature[1]

pleads for a 'many-leveled criticism'[2] to deal with

> all possible levels of meaning in a continuum from the most completely individual, subjective and personal (the unconscious) to the most completely social, objective and impersonal (the historical).[3]

For Kenneth Burke, whom Hyman considers the most outstanding representative of this 'continuum criticism',

> a poem is an act, a symbolic act of the poet who made it – an act of such a nature that in surviving as a structure of object, it enables us as readers to re-enact it.[4]

Here the poem is still called an 'object', but is no longer dissociated from the poet: it embodies the poet's experience which has become an 'act' in it, making it thus possible for us to re-experience it. In other words, it has become a means of communication between poet and reader.

Walter J. Ong discusses how the function of literature as a means of communication is lost in a conception of the poem as an object dissociated from its maker:

> But to consider the work of literature in its primary oral and aural existence, we must enter more profoundly into this world of sound as such, the I–Thou world where, through the mysterious inner resonance which sound best of all provides, persons commune with persons, reaching one another's interiors in a way in which one can never reach the interior of an 'object'.[5]

---

[1] S. E. Hyman, *The Armed Vision*, New York, 1955, p. 3.
[2] *Ibid.* p. 399. [3] *Ibid.* p. 400.
[4] K. Burke, *A Grammar of Motives*, New York, 1945, p. 447.
[5] Ong, *op. cit.* p. 167.

4

If Wellek and Warren reject the view 'that the genuine poem is in the total experience' of its author and add:

> In practice, this conclusion has the serious disadvantage of putting the problem into a completely inaccessible and purely hypothetical X which we have no means of reconstructing or even exploring –[1]

I am inclined to reply: yes, the experience itself *is* inaccessible, and the poem is not 'in' the experience – but is not the poem an accessible part of this experience, in the form of a 'symbolic act'?

Graham Hough, in a recent symposium on literary criticism, has summed up the problem in this way:

> 'Close reading' and the intent scrutiny of the internal structure of poetry was the great pedagogical weapon of the new criticism; and indeed some of it was wanted. But what began as a remedial measure soon became an end in itself, cut off from history, divorced from all natural affections and associations of ordinary reading ... So one comes back with a relief to a style in criticism that was for a time out of fashion: not indeed to chatter about Harriet Shelley, but to the kind of biographical criticism that can see a work in relation to the whole mental and spiritual life of the author.[2]

Perhaps the expression 'biographical criticism' is unfortunate as it tends to conjure up associations just like 'chatter about Harriet Shelley'. If the word 'existential' were not rather over-strained at the moment, I would suggest calling my approach 'existential appreciation': for it tries to understand the poem as an embodiment of the poet's existence.

This does not mean a 'confusion between the poem and its origins', but recognition that the 'origins', that is 'the total experience of the poet during the time of creation', are, to some extent, embodied in the poem. It does not mean an attempt 'to derive the standards of criticism from the psychological causes

[1] Wellek and Warren, *op cit*. p. 149.
[2] G. Hough, 'The Function of the Imagination', *Times Literary Supplement*, 26 July 1963.

of a poem' which would indeed be inadmissible, but an acknowledgement of the fact that, in Walter J. Ong's words,

> in a valid but not exclusive sense, each work of art is not only an object but a kind of surrogate for a person. Anything that bids for attention in an act of contemplation is a surrogate for a person.[1]

VARIOUS APPROACHES TO ELSE LASKER-SCHÜLER

There have been very few large-scale examinations of Else Lasker-Schüler's work, and all of them are dissertations. The most important is that of Margarete Kupper.[2] Her exhaustive research into original texts and sources which she presents as the second part of her thesis and which offers the material for a definitive critical edition of the poet's work is of inestimable value and will have to be considered by any future worker in this field.[3] In the first part of her dissertation which is more relevant to my own enquiry she outlines Else Lasker-Schüler's *Weltanschauung*. Defending her intention to present the *Weltanschauung* of a poet who always insisted that she had none, she pleads with considerable persuasiveness that will and intellect play a greater part in Else Lasker-Schüler's work than is usually granted. Though she does not deny the part played by fantasy and intuition in her 'Dichtung und Weltbild', and admits the existence of an inner necessity, a 'seelisch-geistige Zwangslage',[4] as an important impulse behind her work, her main concern is with this poet's conscious 'decision' to deal with her situation by adopting a certain style of living and writing ('bewußte Selbststilisierung').[5] She discovers in her work, in spite of many contradictions, a consistent concept of life which is essentially religious with a longing for the redemption of a 'heillose' world as its central idea.

[1] Ong, 'The Jinnie in the Well-Wrought Urn', *Essays in Criticism*, London, 1955, p. 319.
[2] M. Kupper, *Die Weltanschauung Else Lasker-Schülers in ihren poetischen Selbstzeugnissen*, Würzburg, 1963.
[3] M. Kupper, 'Materialien zu einer kritischen Ausgabe der Lyrik Else Lasker-Schülers', *Jahrb. der Görres-Gesellschaft*, Neue Folge, IV, 1963.
[4] Kupper, *Weltanschauung*, p. 21.   [5] *Ibid.* p. 21.

The overall structure of Margarete Kupper's examination is very clear; she follows the poet's view of the world throughout the three significant spheres of religion, love and art, and there is a great deal of perceptive and original analysis of detail. But the organization of the material within the three main sections is rather loose, and her conviction that *Weltanschauung* expresses itself even in the order in which the vowels of a poem are arranged does not seem to me sufficiently closely argued to be wholly intelligible. However, anyone attempting an elucidation of Else Lasker-Schüler's work as an entity will have to refer to Margarete Kupper's exposition of the poet's *Weltanschauung*, and I will at a later point return to the way in which I consider my own approach different from hers.

K. J. Höltgen's dissertation[1] offers a profusion of suggestions, ideas and interpretations. At the time of its appearance the collected works of the poet had not yet been published and material about her was even scarcer than it is now. Höltgen, for the first time, tried to give a biographical sketch and raised the problem of the 'Verhältnis von Leben und Werk' which is so fundamental with this writer. He discusses her position as a 'jüdische Dichterin deutscher Zunge', and has a special section on the Kabbalah which he sees as an important influence in her work. He discusses her style, finding it essentially oriental in nature (echoing Meir Wiener's discussion of this subject),[2] examines at some length the principal symbols of her poetry, and ends with interpretations of a selected number of her poems.

Höltgen's dissertation is the work of a pioneer, and as such of great value. But it does not attempt to find a central theme around which its numerous fruitful insights could be ordered into some kind of unified structure.

Sigrid Bauschinger, on the other hand, has found such a theme. In her dissertation *Die Symbolik des Mütterlichen im Werke Else Lasker-Schülers*[3] she has chosen C. G. Jung's theory of archetypes to provide her with a central symbol, the archetype

---

[1] K. J. Höltgen, *Untersuchungen zur Lyrik Else Lasker-Schülers*, Diss., Bonn, 1955.
[2] Meir Wiener, 'Else Lasker-Schüler', in *Juden in der deutschen Literatur*, G. Krojanker, Berlin, 1922.   [3] S. Bauschinger, *op. cit.*

of the Great Mother, in which she sees a key to the symbolic language of the whole range of Else Lasker-Schüler's poetry. With admirable single-mindedness and ingenuity, she interprets not only Earth and Night, but even such non-maternal figures as the [male] Lover and God symbolically in terms of the lost mother for whom the child-poet is in constant search.

This approach, though leading to a number of interesting individual interpretations, is necessarily very restricted. Though Jungians are always ready to accuse Freudians of a tendency to 'reduce' everything to childhood events, they are often blind to their own much more radical 'reductionism'. For while Freudian 'reduction' never leaves the realms of individual history, Jungian insistence on the predominant importance of archetypes is a-historical, and often frankly anti-historical. By stressing what we all have in common, it tends sometimes to neglect what makes each of us specifically what he is. It then leads to statements such as that of Sigrid Bauschinger, in agreement with Heinz Politzer, that the life of Else Lasker-Schüler is without relevance to an understanding of her poetry.

Among the shorter critical examinations of her work, the studies by Walter Muschg, Georg Schlocker and Clemens Heselhaus are the most important. Muschg's chapter on Else Lasker-Schüler in his book on *Dichter des Expressionismus*[1] is the fullest account of her life and work to appear so far, apart from dissertations. Like Höltgen, Muschg offers many ideas and insights, but without a focal point. His most fruitful suggestion seems to me to be that 'Else Lasker-Schüler ist kein "Geschenk des Morgenlandes in deutscher Sprache" . . . sondern ein Erbe der Romantik'.[2] This he elaborates with references to Novalis and Bettina Brentano. His approach, which does not, however, neglect the importance of the Jewish element in her work, balances the extremely one-sided interpretations of Meir Wiener and Heinz Politzer who stress the influence of Jewish tradition to the exclusion of everything else.

[1] W. Muschg, 'Else Lasker-Schüler', *Von Trakl zu Brecht*, Munich, 1961.
[2] *Ibid.* p. 125.

Schlocker's essay touches in a few paragraphs on our own theme, that of Else Lasker-Schüler's 'broken world', and comments on Peter Hille's words about the 'Sappho, der die Welt entzweigegangen ist':

> Der Schmerz um diesen unwiderruflichen Bruch verließ sie nie.[1]

He sees in her 'Gottessehnsucht' an attempt to heal this 'Bruch'. But he does not examine the nature of the split. His essay is meant as an introduction to the work of this poet, in the framework of a symposium on German expressionism, and is thus inevitably fragmentary.

The most important aspect of C. Heselhaus' chapter on Else Lasker-Schüler in his book on modern German poetry is his consideration of her work as breaking new lyrical ground, and his association of her poetry with that of Trakl and Benn:

> Das war eine Rückführung auf die Grundelemente des Lyrischen. Man kann das mit dem Verfahren der Phänomenologie vergleichen, das damals von Husserl entwickelt wurde. Indem man alles abzieht, was rational erklärbar ist, erhält man das Wesen einer Erscheinung. So wurde das Gedicht aller seiner rational-technischen Elemente entkleidet, und zurück blieb das Wesen des Lyrischen: die Ergriffenheit der Lasker-Schüler, die Metapher Trakls, der Rhythmus Benns.[2]

Heselhaus gives her a place in the German Expressionist movement in which he finds the seeds of many characteristics of what we generally call 'modern' in poetry. Höltgen,[3] in his critical comment on Fanni Goldstein's dissertation on Else Lasker-Schüler's 'expressionistischer Stilwille',[4] wonders whether this poet can rightly be seen as a representative of this movement, and Benn himself, in his famous anthology,[5] classes her among

---

[1] G. Schlocker, 'Else Lasker-Schüler', in: *Expressionismus*, ed. H. Friedman and O. Mann, Heidelberg, 1956, p. 140.
[2] C. Heselhaus, 'Else Lasker-Schülers literarisches Traumspiel', *Deutsche Lyrik der Moderne*, Düsseldorf, 1961, p. 214.
[3] *Op. cit.* p. 61ff.
[4] F. Goldstein, *Der expressionistische Stilwille im Werke der Else Lasker-Schüler*, Diss., Vienna, 1936.
[5] *Lyrik des expressionistischen Jahrzehnts*, Wiesbaden, 1955.

the 'forerunners'. We shall return to this question briefly at a later point.

Even this brief survey of the critical assessments of Else Lasker-Schüler's work must not fail to mention the 'footnotes' which Karl Kraus wrote to some poems he published in his *Fackel*. Short though they are, they are of fundamental importance as a great critic's enthusiastic support of the work of a poet then still unrecognized and even ridiculed. Kraus also published in his periodical a review by Richard Weiß of her third collection of poetry, *Meine Wunder*, a penetrating study of her poetic style.[1]

Apart from critical assessments, there are a considerable number of articles and essays of a more personal nature, written by friends and admirers of the poet. They throw a great deal of light on her life, and particularly on how she appeared to her friends and contemporaries, and how they reacted to her. As such they are indispensable to an understanding of her 'world'.

Among these, Werner Kraft's articles and prefaces combine personal impressions of the poet with critical comments on her work. Sigismund von Radetzky's aphoristic 'Erinnerungen' (DD, pp. 575ff.) should also be mentioned here, a series of brief but significant vignettes which evoke Else Lasker-Schüler's personality with loving acuteness.

Finally, there is Catherine Küster-Ginsberg's essay 'Else Lasker-Schüler zum Gedächtnis'[2] in which the author draws on her deep insight into the life and person of the poet whom she befriended in Jerusalem during the last years of her life. In many talks she expanded for me what her essay, which she intended as a kind of verbal 'portrait', implied in its extremely concentrated form. That Else Lasker-Schüler became alive to me as a person and compelled me to ask some questions and attempt some answers, I owe to these talks.

[1] R. Weiß, 'Else Lasker-Schüler', *Die Fackel*, XIII, No. 321/22.
[2] K. Küster, 'Else Lasker-Schüler zum Gedächtnis', *Blick in die Welt*, No. 18, Hamburg, 1948 (all quotations from the original manuscript, which differs from the published article). K. Küster was at the time Catherine Küster-Ginsberg's pen-name.

AIM OF THIS ENQUIRY

The question in which my own approach to Else Lasker-Schüler's poetry found its first crystallization was: what was this poet's 'world', and in what manner had it 'broken apart'? This approach can perhaps be defined by contrasting it with that of Sigrid Bauschinger (see above, pp. 7–8). While she looks for universal 'archetypal' patterns underlying Else Lasker-Schüler's poetry, I am concerned with what this poet specifically *was*, with her own particular 'world', her mode of being, its structure, its split, and with those elements which contained within themselves the possibility of a healing of this split.

Perhaps I can outline my approach even more sharply by comparing it with that of Margarete Kupper. She writes:

> Wohl kommen die sprudelnde Fülle, der Einfallsreichtum ihrer Idee- und Klangassoziationen aus einem unmittelbaren Erlebnisgrund, stellen sich von selbst ein und drängen sich der Dichterin gleichsam auf . . . aber ihr ist dennoch in hohem Maße die Möglichkeit der Kontrolle und des Regulativen gegeben.[1]

If Margarete Kupper is mainly concerned with Else Lasker-Schüler's capacity of conscious 'control' which, as she argues, results in a coherent *Weltanschauung*, my concern is more with what she calls the 'unmittelbaren Erlebnisgrund'. To illustrate this more concretely: Margarete Kupper mentions the contradictions within Else Lasker-Schüler's view of life, she speaks of her vacillation between doubt and faith, her experience of human existence as either 'Geborgenheit' or 'Gefangenschaft', her view of death as either 'Wiedergeburt' or 'erlösendes Ende'[2] – but she does not relate these opposites to each other, does not try to trace their interplay to the very core of this poet's mode of being. I do not wish to say, of course, that Margarete Kupper's argument is lacking in perception but rather that the angle of perception is different. The two approaches seem to me complementary.

[1] M. Kupper, *Die Weltanschauung Else Lasker-Schülers in ihren poetischen Selbstzeugnissen*, Würzburg, 1963, p. 25.   [2] *Ibid.* p. 116.

What then is Else Lasker-Schüler's 'unmittelbarer Erlebnisgrund', what is the structure of her being? It can perhaps be seen as a constant backward and forward swing, an alternation between withdrawal and outgoing, in which the pendulum tended to swing excessively in the one or the other direction.

There was a deep longing for communication, a great readiness for the (in the widest sense) erotic encounter, merging on the highest level into a search for the supreme Thou: God. This wish to give herself, often uncontrolled and indiscriminate, was bound to meet with rebuff and disappointment and then the pendulum swung backwards into isolation and despair. The backward swing showed two extreme manifestations: thoughts of death, of going to die, or of being already dead-in-life; and an escape into fantasy. The escape took many different forms: one was the flight into an idealized childhood, a kind of Golden Age before the Fall; another a tendency to 'dress up', literally and literarily, to hide behind 'masks', to renounce her own identity.

The 'break' in her world was thus one between wish and experience, image and reality. It manifested itself perhaps most strongly in her religious longing where her image of God was again and again clouded and distorted by her inability to bear a reality which she experienced as cold and hostile. But it is in her religious longing also that she came closest to a healing of the split. Throughout her life God became to her increasingly more real, if not more reachable, until in the end she experienced him as someone into whose hands she could trustfully put herself, even though she still did not know who he was.

Else Lasker-Schüler was not unaware of this 'break' in herself though she would perhaps not have interpreted it in the way in which I propose to do. During the last years of her life she wrote a play with the significant title *Ich und Ich* which has the 'split' in her nature as one of its principal themes. Only a few scenes from this play have been published,[1] and they show that 'Versagen der sprachlichen Kraft' (GW, III, 171) which determined Werner Kraft to withhold publication of the complete manuscript. But

---

[1] In GW, III, also in *Hortulus*, X, 1, St Gallen, 1960.

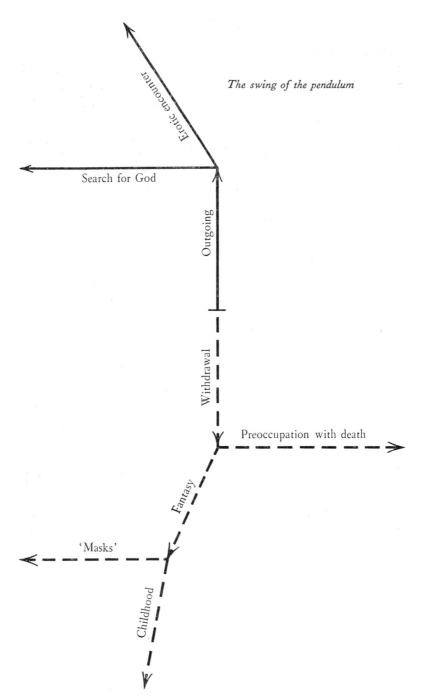

The swing of the pendulum

Erotic encounter

Search for God

Outgoing

Withdrawal

Preoccupation with death

Fantasy

'Masks'

Childhood

even these scenes, in spite of their confusion and incoherence, convey something of the poet's awareness of an inner division which is symbolized by two pairs of protagonists – Faust and Mephisto, the creative and the destructive urge, and the Poetess and Mr Scarecrow, 'das höchste, ewigkeitsnahe und klare ... und das elendeste, verlassene und skurrile Wesen'.[1] Early in the play, the poet announces this division in the manner of a popular ballad:

> Höret, Publikum, die Mordsgeschichte –
> Die ich an mir in finsterer Nacht vollbracht!
> Und da die Wahrheit ich berichte, wenn ich dichte,
> Laßt allen Zweifel außer Acht!
> Es handelt sich nicht etwa – um Gesichte,
> Da ich mich teilte in zwei Hälften kurz vor Tageslichte,
> In zwei Teile: Ich und Ich. (GW, III, 88)

But she goes on to proclaim also the reconciliation of her 'two halves' at least on the stage:

> Da ich und ich im Leben nie zusammenkamen,
> Erreichten meine beiden Hälften dieses kühne
> Rendezvous in kurzer Zeit. (*Ibid.* p. 89)

And the last line of the play hints at how she finally sees the healing of the 'break' – in the affirmation of the presence of God: 'Ich freu mich so, ich freu mich so: Gott ist "da"!' (*ibid.* p. 103).

It is my aim to trace in Else Lasker-Schüler's poetry this division in her being, what I have called the backward and forward movement of the pendulum, and also to show how in her religious poems she came closest to a reconciliation of the conflicting forces.

[1] Kupper, *Weltanschauung*, p. 49.

2. A BIOGRAPHICAL OUTLINE

MYTH AND REALITY

In 1920 the first Expressionist anthology appeared in Berlin, edited by Kurt Pinthus. It contained some poems by Else Lasker-Schüler, and she had also contributed the following autobiographical note:

> Ich bin in Theben (Ägypten) geboren, wenn ich auch in Elberfeld zur Welt kam, im Rheinland. Ich ging bis 11 Jahre zur Schule, wurde Robinson, lebte 5 Jahre im Morgenlande, und seitdem vegetiere ich.[1]

The biographer in search of dates and facts will look at this with dismay, but it does illuminate certain essential aspects of the poet's 'inner' biography. It also shows the particular difficulties which a biographical account of Else Lasker-Schüler presents. Throughout her work, she gives us a great deal of information about herself: but this information, though always significant, is factually unreliable. Astrid Gehlhoff-Claes, in her 'Versuch einer biographischen Darstellung' which forms an appendix to her edition of the poet's letters to Karl Kraus, outlines these difficulties:

> Unmittelbare Rückschlüsse aus den Dichtungen auf Leben und Wesen Else Lasker-Schülers sind jedoch oft Kurzschlüsse. Man muß sich hüten, Einzelheiten wörtlich zu nehmen und auf eine objektive Wahrheit der Berichte zu bauen ... Wir wissen heute, daß Else Lasker-Schüler mit Absicht die Spuren ihres Lebensweges verwischt hat ... Neben der bewußten Verschleierung und Veränderung ist die unbewußte Verwandlung des Wirklichen unter dem Einfluß der schöpferischen Phantasie zu berücksichtigen.
>
> (BK, pp. 141, 142)

This blurring of the borderline between 'Dichtung und Wahrheit', fantasy and reality, was an aspect of the very structure of Else Lasker-Schüler's life. It is one of the aims of this enquiry to examine its roots.

---

[1] Kurt Pinthus, *Menschheitsdämmerung*, Berlin, 1920, p. 294.

Looking more closely at this autobiographical note, we can distinguish some principal themes. The first sentence expresses her involvement with origins, with the past in general and more particularly with her birth, but also the tension between reality (Elberfeld) and fantasy (Theben). It points to her sense of disorientation in the actual world and her longing for an ideal state of being for which the East and the biblical past became two prominent symbols.

The second sentence presents us with the problem of dates. We do not know whether she did, in fact, leave school when she was eleven. In one of her numerous autobiographical essays she describes a traumatic experience which led to illness and inter-ruption of schooling (GW, II, 699); but we do not know whether even this description corresponds to reality. Nevertheless, we shall have to concern ourselves with it: for the very fact that she describes these events throws light on her 'inner' biography, whether they really happened or not. Again: what do '5 Jahre im Morgenlande' mean? I assume that they indicate the time between her leaving school and her first marriage. She speaks of this marriage as a disaster from which she never quite recovered: 'Ich fiel ins Haus und verletzte mir die Knie, die bluten seitdem' (GW, II, 179) – words which seem to be echoed by the expression 'seitdem vegetiere ich'. In another autobiographical account, she speaks of having married when she was sixteen.[1] However, the dates do not work: even if one took as a basis for calculation the date she gave as that of her birth, 1876 (instead of the real date which was 1869), she would have been eighteen when she married in 1894, and not sixteen. Her attitude towards age, about which more will have to be said, is summed up by Gehlhof-Claes: 'Else Lasker-Schüler wollte kein zählbares Alter haben, sie wollte zeitlos sein' (BK, p. 145). She wanted to transform her life into a myth, and a myth is timeless.

The key word in the second sentence of this note is 'Robinson'; it symbolizes not only her feeling of isolation, of being 'ship-wrecked' without any human contact, which, as we shall see,

---

[1] E. Kern (ed.), *Führende Frauen Europas in 25 Selbstschilderungen*, Munich, n.d., p. 14.

is a constantly recurring theme of her work, but also her need for constructing out of whatever the sea of her imagination washed ashore a world of her own in order to survive.

The inspection of this passage (only one of many similar ones) has demonstrated both the difficulties and the opportunities which the autobiographical part of her writings offers. We have seen the unreliability of the ostensibly factual material: it needs careful checking which, at the present moment, is often impossible, since there is still too little reliable information available. But we have also seen that even this short note spotlights several important themes: her feeling of isolation, her escape into the past and fantasy, her determination to present her life as a myth.

In the following I shall try to establish the external outline of her life, using such dates and facts as are at present accessible. This will serve as an outer frame for the 'inner' biography which is my main concern.

CHILDHOOD

Else Lasker-Schüler was born on 11 February 1869 in Wuppertal-Elberfeld. This is the date entered at the Registry Office, but the birth certificate was only found recently, and until then the year 1876 had been accepted as the year of her birth. It seems that she herself gave this wrong date at the time of her second marriage to Herwarth Walden who was ten years younger than herself. Gehlhoff-Claes rejects the obvious explanation of this falsification (BK, p. 144), and it does indeed seem necessary to see the poet's attitude towards her age as an aspect of her need to turn her life into fantasy. Schalom Ben-Chorin, in an article about his meeting with her in Jerusalem in 1937, tells how violently she reacted to the celebration of her sixtieth birthday by the press. She wrote to him:

> Ich bin erstens nicht so alt, und es *schädigt* mich ja wieder . . . Ich wünsche, daß Sie irgendwie in einem Artikel erwähnen, daß Sie sich im Alter geirrt haben, *ich* [bin] wohl 1000 und wäre aber auch 20 Jahre. Wollen Sie mich total vernichten?[1]

[1] Sch. Ben-Chorin, 'Prinz Jussuf in Jerusalem', *Tribüne*, 1, 3, 1962, p. 304.

Her father, Aron Schüler, was the grandson of a rabbi (who as the Chief Rabbi of the Rhineland and Westphalia figures in her play *Arthur Aronymus* and her story *Der Wunderrabbiner von Barcelona*) and the son of Moses Schüler who according to Gehlhoff-Claes was a gentleman farmer (BK, p. 146), according to Springmann a merchant.[1]

Aron Schüler was, in fact, a private banker. But Else Lasker-Schüler writes about him throughout as if he had been an architect, and this is how he is still described in most reference books. Springmann mentions that Aron Schüler had business connections with the building trade,[2] and we can thus trace the seed from which the myth has grown.

The father as a builder of towers appears in a number of her autobiographical references, e.g.

> Mit Vorliebe beschäftigte sich mein Vater mit dem Bauen der Häuser, namentlich der Aussichtstürme der Stadt und ihrer Umgegend, die sich immer zu hoch verstiegen, jedenfalls der Nachbarschaft Sorge für Haus und Hof, der Herbststürme eingedenk, verursachten. (GW, II, 533)

> Mit welcher Begeisterung mein Vater seine Türme erbaute, sie mitten in der Stadt hinsetzte oder wie den unsrigen liebevoll an die grüne Seite des großen Hauses lehnte, zählt zu meiner Kindheit liebsten Erinnerung. (GW, II, 872)

She describes her father as a boisterous, playful, humorous and rather violent person.

> Mein Vater war der ausgelassenste Mensch gewesen, den ich je im Leben kennengelernt habe, einen Schelm hatte er immer wo auf dem Polster seines roten Herzens sitzen. Er war beileibe nicht frohgemut aus Tiefe . . . er war ausgelassen aus Breite. Er strömte, er brandete, er zerstörte . . . (GW, II, 748)

This portrait is not unlike that drawn by eyewitnesses and quoted by Springmann:

> Er muß nach Berichten von Augenzeugen ein großes Original gewesen sein. So berichtete ein verstorbener Zeitgenosse von

---

[1] W. Springmann (ed.), *Else Lasker-Schüler und Wuppertal*, Wuppertal-Elberfeld, 1962 p.12.　　[2] *Ibid.* p. 13.

ihm, wie er durch die Aue gekommen sei und laut die Börsenkurse
heraustrompetet habe, umringt von einer jauchzenden Kohorte
von Gassenbuben, denen der dabei Bonbons verteilt habe.[1]

She thought of her father as the originator of her passion for
toys and play:

> Obendrein ich eine Spiellust geerbt hab' sondergleichen;
> wahrscheinlich nur meinem Vater zum Vorwand geboren bin,
> noch in seinen weißen Jahren die Spielware der Läden, mich
> vorschiebend, unauffällig betrachten zu können.   (GW, II, 678)

Once she refers to her father and herself as 'wir zwei Kinder'
(GW, II, 747) and he emerges altogether as a lovable but not
quite grown-up eccentric. Though he plays a great part in her
prose-writings, he does not appear in her poems at all (except
by implication where she mentions her parents). It seems that
she was unable to take him quite seriously, though she found
herself drawn towards a playfulness which was so much like
her own. One cannot help wondering to what extent the image
of her father disturbed her future relationships with men.

While memories of her father are confined to her prose writings, her mother is one of the dominating figures and symbols
of her poetry. Jeannette Kissing was the daughter of a wine-
merchant who had come from Spain by way of England to
Southern Germany where he had married Johanna Kopp whom
Else Lasker-Schüler describes as 'die wunderschöne Dichterin'
(GW, II, 532), though there is no evidence that her grandmother
did, in fact, write poetry. It is more likely that, by another touch
of fantastic elaboration, she wishes to emphasize her conviction
that her poetic inspiration was a maternal gift:

> Schlage ich meiner Mama Poesiealbum auf und betrachte der
> Worte südliche Buchstaben, Gedichte aus seltenen holden
> Knospen und seidigen Blättern geschrieben, weiß ich, 'sie' war
> die Dichterin und ich nur die Sagerin ihrer reinen schwärmerischen
> Gedanken.   (GW, II, 876)

She felt that it was her mother who first recognized her poetic
talent. She describes mother's reaction when as a child she told

---

[1] Springmann, *op. cit.* p. 13.

her about her fantasies around a lit bay-window – 'Du bist eine Dichterin' (GW, II, 708). It was also her mother who obtained for her the coloured buttons with which she loved to play, making patterns in which she later saw her first poetic creations:

> Ob man mit grünen, lila und blauen Steinen spielt oder ob man dichtet, das ist ganz dasselbe. (BK, p. 11)

She also describes rhyming-games which her mother played with her and her sisters when she was only two, and stresses her own sensitivity to bad rhymes (GW, II, 518). She tells how mother found her first poems in her pockets when she was five:

> Fünfjährig dichtete ich meine besten Gedichte; meine Mutter fand immer die bekritzelten Papierflocken, die mir aus meinem Kleidertäschchen beim Herausholen von Lieblingsknöpfen meiner Knopfsammlung entkamen. (GW, II, 518)

Mother seems to have been, in many ways, the opposite of father – 'eine feine und anfällige, zur Melancholie neigende Frau', as Gehlhoff-Claes describes her (BK, p. 147). Else Lasker-Schüler speaks about her always with deep affection, and sometimes with an almost ecstatic admiration:

> Ich liebte meine Mama inbrünstig, sie war meine Freundin, mein Heiligenbild, meine Stärkung, meine Absolution, mein Kaiser. (GW, II, 597)

> Mein Herz blüht auf, wenn ich an meine Mutter denke. Ich habe kein Geheimnis vor ihr, sie nahm mich mit sich von der Erde fort, sie blieb in meinem Herzen hier auf der Welt... (GW, II, 410)

Her deep involvement with her mother is shown by the incident which she relates in 'Der letzte Schultag' and to which I have already referred (see above, p. 16). She describes how one day mother went for a walk and did not return, and how everyone went to look for her. She herself climbed the tower of the house, and from there she saw her mother coming down the hill, 'so traurig, das vermag meine Hand nicht zu schildern', and in order to reach her quickly, the child jumped from the tower, but was fortunately caught by the sun blind which stretched out in front of the window underneath – 'denn Kinder haben alle einen besonderen Schutzengel'. She goes on to tell how she was saved by the fire brigade, developed St Vitus' Dance (owing to the shock, as the doctor said – but she herself thought the worry about mother responsible for it) and did not return to school (GW, II, 699).

As I have said before, we do not know whether this incident did in fact take place. But even if she only invented it, it would still throw some light on her great dependence on her mother which, as we shall see, was such an important factor in shaping her development.

Else Lasker-Schüler was twenty-one when her mother died. It was a deep shock which she never quite overcame. 'Wie meine Mutter starb, zerbrach der Mond' (GW, II, 758). She kept her alive in herself and in her poetry as a kind of inspiring angel with whom she felt in constant contact. Even at the end of her life, she could still write:

> Es brennt die Kerze auf meinem Tisch
> Für meine Mutter die ganze Nacht –
> Für meine Mutter (. . .)   (GW, I, 333)

Else Lasker-Schüler was one of six children, three boys and three girls. We do not know a great deal about her relationship with her brothers and sisters, except that with her brother Paul who was the youngest of the boys and eight years older than herself. Him she loved and idolized:

> Mein Bruder war ein junger König, ein Mönch, der Himmel sein
> blauer Dom.   (GW, II, 604)

> Mein Bruder Paul besuchte auch noch die Schule, das Gymnasium, er dichtete lateinisch und griechisch, meine teure Mutter und er lasen sich heimlich im Wohnzimmer gegenseitig ihre Gedichte vor. Mir half er bei meinen Schularbeiten (. . .) Er kannte alle Bäume und Sträucher und Blumen, als ob er mit Gott die Welt geschaffen habe. 'Zugegen war er sicher', meinte auf dem Schulhof meine Freundin Emmy, 'da er ein Heiliger ist, ein Apollon.'
>
>   (GW, II, 746)

21

Once more we meet here her need to turn reality into legend by mixing fact and fantasy. In the pantheon of semi-divine figures which she created as a kind of sanctuary from the threats of actuality her brother Paul had a special place. He died when he was only twenty-two, and she gave his name to her own son who also was to die early and whom she idolized in a similar way.

MARRIAGE

Else Lasker-Schüler married twice, but both marriages broke down. Her mythical interpretation of these marriages is contained in an autobiographical sketch which she contributed to Elga Kern's collection *Führende Frauen Europas* (see also above, p. 16). There she writes:

> Einmal beim Unterricht lag eine Riesenschlange auf dem Boden des Zimmers, darin ich ochsen mußte. Wer sie hingelegt hatte, kam erst nach Jahren heraus. Natürlich handelte es sich um einen Racheakt, denn ich hatte einem kleinen Spielgefährten im Räuber- und Gendarmspiel in der Erregung die Nase abgebissen. Seitdem habe ich eine Aversion vor Schleicherei. Darum entschloß ich mich, als ich sechzehn Jahre alt war, eine Marderart zu heiraten, die die Schlangen zu töten pflegt (. . .) Als die letzte Schlange aus der Welt geschafft war, heiratete ich einen blonden Menschen, der momentan sich davon ernährt, meine Manuskripte (fehlende Gedichte ersetzt er) an Antiquitätenhändler zu verkaufen. Meine dritte Heirat – darüber möchte ich nicht sprechen, man könnte ihn mir sonst abspenstig machen.

The account of her first marriage given here sounds like a dream, and without the associations of the dreamer it is difficult to interpret. It seems that she expected her first husband to protect her from 'Schleicherei', that is, false friendliness under which malice is hidden as the snake in the grass, a tendency she hated all her life with a passionate hatred which appears here to be rooted in some painful childhood experience. Why she thought Dr Lasker capable of 'killing' this threat, we are not told. The sentence referring to her second husband, Herwarth Walden, expresses unusual contempt and throws out a grave accusation without substantiating it. The last sentence indicates her ever-present wish to find some day the right partner, and also her fear that the world would destroy such a partnership. The whole passage is a particularly striking example of her need to 'mask' reality.

She was not sixteen but twenty-four when she married J. B. Lasker, a doctor practising in Berlin. This marriage and the move to the capital meant a complete break with her comparatively sheltered, family-bound, way of life in a provincial town. We do not know exactly why this marriage failed: Springmann[1] speaks of Lasker's petit-bourgeois background by which she felt herself imprisoned; and Gehlhoff-Claes (BK, p. 151) mentions that even Lasker's closest friends did not know that he was married. There are no details known about how the marriage ended, but when it did, it marked the beginning of the Bohemian manner of life, without a permanent home and with insufficient means, which – with many variations – was to be hers for the rest of her life.

In 1899 she met 'auf der Straße' Alcibiades de Rouan, a Greek, with whom she seems to have been very much in love and who, after the collapse of her marriage, was her 'einzige große Freude'. Their son, Paul, was born a year later. This episode remains shrouded in mystery: the few facts put down here are mentioned by Gehlhoff-Claes to whom they were told by Friedja Schugt, a friend of the poet (BK, p. 151 and notes, p. 78).

In 1899 and 1900 she published her first poems in the magazines *Die Gesellschaft* and *Das Magazin für Literatur*. These poems, though very immature and derivative, already tried to give voice to themes that were to remain important.

In 1901 she married the writer and composer Georg Levin, who as Herwarth Walden (a name she herself is said to have given him) became one of the leaders and theoreticians of the German Expressionist Movement. In 1910 he founded *Der Sturm*, which beside Pfempfert's *Aktion* was the most important of the early Expressionist periodicals and published many of Else Lasker-Schüler's poems. In 1911 the marriage was dissolved.

[1] Springmann, *op. cit.* p. 86.

Gehlhoff-Claes (*ibid.* pp. 154ff.) devotes some space to discussing the reasons for the failure of this marriage. She rejects the attempts made by various writers to take Else Lasker-Schüler's own description of her relation with Walden in *Mein Herz* as a valid basis for understanding. There she had written to Walden:

> Ich kenn Dich und Du kennst mich, wir können uns nicht mehr überraschen, und ich kann nur leben von Wundern. (GW, II, 314)

From this the conclusion was drawn that it was her inability to relate truly and permanently to another person – what Muschg calls her 'erotic anarchism'[1] – that destroyed the marriage. Against this, Gehlhoff-Claes stresses the fictional character of *Mein Herz* which made it unsuitable as biographical material, and quotes the testimony of the poet's friends to show that it was Walden who ended the marriage. She also quotes, in this context, a letter to Kraus in which she writes:

> Ich selbst . . . bin schon lange mit Herwarth auseinander; er hat sich schon lange verliebt gehabt in eine Schwedin . . . aber ich durfte nie etwas sagen ohne eine unbequeme Stimmung hervorzubeschwören. (BK, p. 47)

Gehlhoff-Claes also quotes other letters which show that she defended Walden when he was attacked.

While it is certainly true that hasty judgment will not lead to an understanding of this complex situation, it cannot be denied (and will have to be examined in greater detail) that Else Lasker-Schüler had deep-seated difficulties in making contact with others and a romantic image of love which was fated to clash with reality. Also, *Mein Herz*, an epistolary novel made up mainly of a number of letters addressed to Walden (who at the time was in Norway with a friend), though as little reliable as a source of information as the rest of her prose writings, is at the same time by no means devoid of biographical significance. Here again the distinction between 'outer' and 'inner' biography must be made.

While married to Walden, she published her first two volumes of poetry, *Styx* (1902) and *Der Siebente Tag* (1905). During this

---

[1] Muschg, *op. cit.* p. 122.

time also there appeared her first two books of prose: a book in memory of her friend and teacher, the strange poet-prophet Peter Hille who had died in 1904 and whom she 'canonizes' as 'St. Peter' in a number of legendary episodes (*Das Peter Hille-Buch*, 1906), and a collection of oriental fantasies (*Die Nächte der Tino von Bagdad*, 1907) in which she presents herself in the first of her 'masks', that of an Eastern princess. In 1909, her first play, *Die Wupper*, was published, though it was not performed until ten years later.

Her connection, through Walden, with the *Sturm*-circle raises the question whether she can be considered a representative of the Expressionist movement. As we have seen (see above, p. 9), there has been some doubt about this. There are, of course, a great many different definitions of Expressionism by a great many different writers, and for this very reason the justification of such definitions has sometimes been questioned. However, it seems to me that, within certain limits and as long as it is not misused as a label, the term 'Expressionism' describes a definite and concrete poetic aim. G. Wilpert defines it as a 'Reaktion der Seele . . . gegen die materielle Wirklichkeitsnachbildung im Naturalismus und die Wiedergabe äußerer Eindrücke im Impressionismus . . .', and proceeds to characterize the Expressionist method in this way:

> Künstlerische Gestaltung folgt nunmehr als reiner geistiger Ausdruck innerlich geschauter Wahrheiten und seelischer Erlebnisse des Ich unter freier Benutzung der äußeren Gegebenheiten (Natur, Sprache) . . .[1]

If we apply this characterization to the work of Else Lasker-Schüler, we cannot doubt that she can rightly be called an Expressionist poet, and Fritz Martini seems to make this application when he writes about her:

> Expressionistisch ist die Einverwandlung der Landschaft, die Vermenschlichung aller Dinge, ihre Teilnahme, ja Identität mit dem Ich.[2]

[1] G. Wilpert, *Sachwörterbuch der Literatur*, Stuttgart, 1955, p. 160.
[2] F. Martini, *Was war Expressionismus?*, Urach, 1948, p. 110.

Similarly, Richard Weiß, in one of the earliest critical estimates of her poetry, writes:

> Die Seele selbst ist der Schauplatz geworden, dessen Geschehen in den Dimensionen der Welt ausgedrückt wird.[1]

This is not only an acute characterization of her work – it sums up the very essence of Expressionism itself.

FRIENDS

During the three years after her divorce from Walden she met three men who, in varying degree, were to play an important part in her life: Franz Marc, Gottfried Benn and Georg Trakl.

She seems to have met Marc in 1912, the year after her divorce and also the year when her third volume of poetry, *Meine Wunder*, appeared. Maria Marc tells how she and her husband had been impressed by the poems which had appeared in *Der Sturm* and how they had longed to make Else Lasker-Schüler's acquaintance. When they came to Berlin, they saw her in the Café Josty, but as they were sharing a table with Walden and his second wife, while Else Lasker-Schüler was sitting with friends at another table, no contact was yet made: she and Walden were at the time no longer on speaking-terms. Eventually they visited her, and as they found her unwell, they invited her to their house.

> Aber weder als Gast in unserem Hause, noch in einem hübschen Zimmer, das wir für sie gefunden hatten, mit weiter Aussicht über das Moor bis zu den Bergen, fühlte sie sich wohl . . . Es kam nur noch größere Unruhe über die arme Seele. Sie fühlte sich verloren in der Weite und flüchtete sich wieder in die Stadt, nach München, in eine enge Pension. Als wir sie dort besuchten, fanden wir sie in ihrem Zimmer an einem Tisch voller Zinnsoldaten, mit denen sie heftige Kämpfe ausfocht – an Stelle der Kämpfe, die ihr Leben ihr beständig brachte.[2]

[1] R. Weiß, 'Else Lasker-Schüler', *Die Fackel*, XIII, No. 321/22, p. 45.
[2] Maria Marc, *Franz Marc, Botschaften an den Prinzen Jussuf*, Munich, 1954, pp. 6–7.

This account shows something of her restlessness, and also of the way in which she escaped from reality into play.

She felt a great affinity to Marc. 'In seinen Bildern fand sie die eigene Ehrfurcht vor dem göttlichen Leben in aller Kreatur wieder' (BK, p. 160). In her prose-poem *Franz Marc* she wrote about his death in the First World War:

> Er ist gefallen. Seinen Riesenkörper tragen große Engel zu Gott, der hält seine blaue Seele, eine leuchtende Fahne, in seiner Hand (...) Nie sah ich irgendeinen Maler gotternster und sanfter malen wie ihn. (GW, I, 270)

She wrote a number of letters to him which were published from 1913 to 1917 in the periodicals *Die Aktion*, *Der Brenner* (which also published Trakl's poetry) and *Neue Jugend*, and were then collected and published in 1919 under the title *Der Malik. Eine Kaisergeschichte*. Marc answered these letters by sending her a number of postcards, on which he painted animals: horses, deer and panthers in delicate blue and red colours.

In 1912 she also met Gottfried Benn. She fell passionately in love with him, but what he felt for her at the time is less clear. Forty years later he said:

> Im heutigen Berlin bin ich wahrscheinlich einer der wenigen, die Else Lasker-Schüler persönlich kannten, sicher auch der einzige, dem sie eine Zeitlang sehr nahestand, vermutlich auch der einzige, der am Grabe ihres Sohnes Paul stand.[1]

Walter Lennig characterizes the relationship rather laconically like this:

> Die kurze Liebesbeziehung zu der Dichterin Else Lasker-Schüler war eher melancholisch als glücklich.[2]

F. W. Wodtke, in his bibliographical study of Benn, mentions the autumn of 1913 as the probable date of their separation, 'nach einer mißglückten Begegnung auf Hiddensee'. But all this remains in the realms of speculation. More important is Wodtke's

---

[1] G. Benn, *Gesammelte Werke*, II, Wiesbaden, 1959, p. 537.
[2] W. Lennig, *Gottfried Benn in Selbstzeugnissen und Bilddokumenten*, Hamburg, 1962, p. 28.

suggestion that some of Benn's poetry at the time was influenced by that of Else Lasker-Schüler: 'Die ins Surreal-Visionäre gesteigerte Sprache und Bildlichkeit dieser neuen Gedichte sind stark von der Lyrik der Lasker-Schüler bestimmt.' (He thinks particularly of *Ein Mann spricht*, *Drohung*, and *Madonna*.)[1]

Else Lasker-Schüler herself describes the flaring up of her love for Benn (whom she called Giselheer, renaming him as she did all her friends) in some letters to Marc contained in *Der Malik*:

> Ich hab mich doch wirklich wieder verliebt. (. . .) Er heißt Giselheer. Sein Gehirn ist ein Leuchtturm. Er ist aus den Nibelungen.
>
> (GW, II, 401)

The following letter already describes the end:

> Du freust Dich über meine neue 'Liebe'. – Du sagst das so leicht hin and ahnst nicht, daß Du eher mit mir weinen müßtest – denn – sie ist schon verloschen in seinem Herzen, wie ein bengalisches Feuer, ein brennendes Rad – es fuhr mal eben über mich.
>
> (GW, II, 402)

In a short essay 'Doktor Benn' she draws a perceptive and evocative portrait of the poet of *Morgue* and of *Söhne* (which was dedicated to her):

> Er steigt hinunter ins Gewölbe seines Krankenhauses und schneidet die Toten auf. Ein Nimmersatt, sich zu bereichern an Geheimnis (. . .) Lang bevor ich ihn kannte, war ich seine Leserin; sein Gedichtbuch – Morgue – lag auf meiner Decke: Grauenvolle Kunstwunder, Todesträumerei, die Kontur annahm (. . .) Jeder seiner Verse ein Leopardbiß, ein Wildtiersprung. Der Knochen ist sein Griffel, mit dem er das Wort auferweckt.
>
> (GW, II, 227–8)

Benn retained a great regard for her to the end of his life. In a letter to Astrid Gehlhoff-Claes he wrote:

> Jedes Gedicht an alle die Männer und Frauen war echt. Sie spuckte auf alles Unechte.[2]

[1] F. W. Wodtke, *Gottfried Benn*, Stuttgart, 1962, p. 15.
[2] G. Benn, *Das gezeichnete Ich. Briefe aus den Jahren 1900–1956*, Munich, 1962, p. 149.

And in 1953 he introduced an evening devoted to a reading of her work with a short speech which is one of the most moving tributes ever paid to her:

> Und dies war die größte Lyrikerin, die Deutschland je hatte. Mir persönlich sagte sie immer, sagt sie auch heute mehr als die Droste, als Sophie Merrau oder Ricarda Huch. Ihre Themen waren vielfach jüdisch, ihre Phantasie orientalisch, aber ihre Sprache war deutsch, ein üppiges, prunkvolles, zartes Deutsch, eine Sprache reif und süß, in jeder Wendung dem Kern des Schöpferischen entsprossen.[1]

We do not know much about her relation with Georg Trakl whom she met very shortly before he died. Wolfgang Schneditz, in an essay on Trakl, describes how the poet met her in February 1914 in Berlin where he had come to find help for his sister who was thought to be dying after an abortion.[2] Trakl was deeply and, it seems now certain, incestuously involved with his sister,[3] and therefore at the time in a state of great disturbance and despair. Schneditz assumes that in Else Lasker-Schüler he met someone to whom he could talk. But he gives no details of the meeting. That she felt sympathetic towards Trakl's emotional difficulties, this comment, quoted by Werner Kraft, shows:

> Und wenn auch, ich habe mir immer einen Bruder als Geliebten gewünscht, da weiß man doch wenigstens, was man hat, und man braucht sich nicht zu verachten. (GW, III, 160)

Else Lasker-Schüler wrote two poems about Trakl, one a kind of epitaph:

> Georg Trakl erlag im Krieg von eigener Hand gefällt.
> So einsam war es in der Welt. Ich hatt ihn lieb. (GW, I, 255)

Longer than her association with Marc, Benn and Trakl was her friendship with Karl Kraus. Gehlhoff-Claes, in her edition of the poet's letters to Kraus, does not tell us when and how these

---

[1] G. Benn, *Werke*, I, p. 538.
[2] W. Schneditz, *Georg Trakl*. In: Georg Trakl, *Gesammelte Werke*, II, p. 87.
[3] Th. Spoerri, *Georg Trakl*, Bern, 1954, p. 41.

two met. The first of these letters is dated 1909, the last 1923. Clashes and disagreements between such dissimilar personalities – the intellectual, fastidious critic, and the intuitive, impulsive poet – were, of course, inevitable, but it seems that it was, in the end, his indifference towards her son Paul that disrupted their friendship. In her last letter, she writes:

> Da Sie mein Kind nicht *einmal* einluden, ja dafür hasse ich Sie
> und nichts in der Welt versöhnt mich.   (BK, p. 100)

This letter was headed 'Mein verehrter Herr Kraus' – like some others preceding it during the period 1915 to 1922 when letters became much less frequent and less warm – while during the time of greater closeness, Kraus was 'Verehrter Cardinal', 'Lieber Herzog von Wien' or 'Lieber Dalai Lama', a many-faced but always important figure in her mythology.

She had an acute appreciation of Kraus's integrity as a critic of society:

> Er bohrt Höhlen in den Samt des Vorhangs, der die Schäden
> verschleiert schwer. (. . .) Mit ruhiger Papsthand klappt er das
> Schachbrett zusammen, mit dem die Welt zugenagelt ist.
>
> (GW, II, 226–7)

But she was also aware of his limitations as a person:

> Ich würde Sie nie (. . .) je ins Meulwerk des Spiessers laßen auf
> Gefahr meines Lebens hin, *aber ich sage Ihnen was wären Sie wenn*
> *Sie inniger wären.*   (BK, p. 99)

Karl Kraus recognized the greatness of her poetry, published some of it in his periodical *Die Fackel*, as long as he still published anything he had not written himself (when he no longer did so, she was unable to accept it!), and wrote deeply appreciative critical notes about it:

> Ich halte Else Lasker-Schüler für eine große Dichterin. Ich
> halte alles, was um sie herum neugetönt wird, für eine Frechheit.[1]

[1] *Fackel*, No. 351–3, June 1912.

About her poem *Ein alter Tibetteppich* he wrote:

> Das hier . . . zitierte Gedicht gehört für mich zu den entzückend-
> sten und ergreifendsten, die ich je gelesen habe. Und wenige
> von Goethe abwärts gibt es, in denen so wie in diesem Tibetteppich
> Sinn und Klang, Wort und Bild, Sprache und Seele verwoben sind.[1]

In 1913, when she was in great financial difficulties, he published an appeal in the *Fackel* for contributions to relieve her
poverty; this was signed by a number of famous people, among
them Selma Lagerlöf, Dehmel and Schönberg.

Between 1911 and 1914, she published, apart from *Mein
Herz*, the 'Briefroman' which was an augmented edition of her
'Briefe nach Norwegen' that had appeared in *Der Sturm*, two
further books of prose: a volume of essays, *Gesichte* (1913),
and *Der Prinz von Theben. Ein Geschichtenbuch* (1914), in which
she presented herself in a new 'mask', that of Jussuf, a kind of
re-incarnation of the biblical Joseph. (The importance of these
'masks' will be discussed later.) At this time also, her *Hebräische
Balladen* (1913) appeared.

The time between 1914 and 1927 is not marked by any striking
external events. In 1917, an edition of her *Gesammelte Gedichte*
appeared. (There were to be two more editions, the last in 1920
in two volumes.) In 1919, her letters to Marc were published under
the title *Der Malik*; here again she figures as 'Jussuf, Prinz von
Theben'. In the same year the first performance of *Die Wupper*
took place in Reinhardt's 'Deutsches Theater'. (The play was
to see two more performances: in 1927 in Berlin, and in 1958 in
Cologne.)

In 1925 friends organized another collection to relieve the financial stress under which Else Lasker-Schüler was almost constantly
suffering. During all this time, she lived a Bohemian kind of
life, spending a great deal of time in the café which she both
loved and loathed ('Heimlich halten wir alle das Café für den
Teufel, aber ohne den Teufel ist doch nun mal nichts.' GW, II,
298), counting many of the literary and artistic celebrities of the
day among her friends.

[1] *Ibid.* No. 313–14, December 1910.

PAUL

In 1927, her son Paul died in Lugano, twenty-seven years old, of tuberculosis. Sigismund von Radetzky gives a most moving description of his death:

> Als er fühlte, daß es jetzt ans Sterben ging, gab er der Mutter ein Zeichen, hinter den Vorhang zu treten; er wollte allein sterben. Gehorsam trat sie hinter den Vorhang und wartete dort den Tod ihres Sohnes ab. (DD, p. 579)

To this son she was more attached than to any other living being. She was also deeply aware of her own shortcomings as a mother. Paul, a gifted artist (Franz Marc himself was ready to teach him), showed a great deal of his mother's restlessness, and Else Lasker-Schüler blamed herself for this. Her feelings of guilt increased after his death and were never to leave her. Thus, Rachel Katinka, who met her towards the end of her life in Jerusalem, writes:

> Und dann sprach sie mir von ihrem einzigen Sohn. Sie sprach über das Bohemeleben, das er führte, sprach von sich selbst, wie sie nicht verstanden hatte, Mutter zu sein und ihn zu behüten, erzählte von seinem Sterben und weinte bitterlich. (DD, pp. 595f.)

Even six years after his death she wrote to a friend that she was unable to travel through Lugano 'des Schmerzes wegen' (DD, p. 544).

She seems to have hoped that Paul would realize something of her own potentialities. About this she wrote to Karl Kraus:

> Was in mir verwischt und verdorrt, verknorpelt ist unter der Härte im Kampf mit der furchtbaren, nüchteren Menschheit, blüht in Paul viel prachtvoller auf. (BK, p. 84)

In her *Nachlaß*, there is a letter to 'Mein geliebtes kleines Päulchen', written in Jerusalem in 1939, which shows how little she had accepted her son's death:

> Du hast mir im Traum gesagt, und ich habe in Deinem Wunsch die große Sehnsucht empfunden, mein geliebtes kleines Päulchen, –

ich soll Dir doch einen Brief schreiben. Wo Du auch gerade bist, mein Päulchen, ich sehe Dich immer, Dich und meine Mama, Euch beide inniglich zusammen. (. . .) Einmal hast Du mir gesagt im Wachen: 'Das ist so: Ich heiße der Engel Paul.' Alles habe ich genau gehört und verstanden, mein Kind.　　(GW, III, 11)

Death also was a reality which she had often to turn into fantasy in order to be able to bear it and live with it.

EMIGRATION

In 1932 Else Lasker-Schüler received the 'Kleist-Preis'. In the same year, her most important book of essays, *Konzert*, appeared, which contains the majority of pieces dealing with her childhood. Also in 1932, the story *Arthur Aronymus* which she called 'Die Geschichte meines Vaters' was published as well as its dramatization. A performance of the play was planned in Darmstadt for 1933, but the arrival of the Nazi regime prevented this. In 1933 she emigrated to Switzerland.

Her feelings about this as well as her great love for Germany are expressed in the poem *Die Verscheuchte* which starts

> Es ist der Tag im Nebel völlig eingehüllt
> Entseelt begegnen alle Welten sich –

and later has the lines

> Ich streife heimatlos zusammen mit dem Wild
> Durch bleiche Zeiten träumend – ja ich liebte dich . . .
>
> (GW, I, 347)

Of this poem, a number of versions are in existence. One is in possession of Dr Job in Zürich; there it has the title *Das Lied der Emigrantin*, and its three final lines, which are missing in the printed version, convey more strongly her feelings about Germany at this moment:

> Und deine Lippe, die der meinen glich,
> Ist wie ein Pfeil nun blind auf mich gezielt.
> Und alles starb, was ich für dich gefühlt.　(GW, I, 412, note)

Between 1933 and 1940, she led the unsettled life of a refugee. In 1934 she went to Alexandria and made her first journey to Palestine. She returned to Switzerland, where in 1936 the first performance of *Arthur Aronymus* took place in Zürich. The following year she went again to Palestine, and her impressions resulted in the book *Das Hebräerland*, in which she substituted her own image of the country for the much less harmonious reality she had met. In 1940 she went to Palestine for the third time, and this time she settled in Jerusalem.

JERUSALEM

Else Lasker-Schüler tells us in *Das Hebräerland* that even as a child she liked to draw Jerusalem (GW, II, 907). 'Unsere heilige Stadt im Herrn' (GW, I, 319) meant to her much more than just a geographical place, the capital of a new state:

> Gott baute aus Seinem Rückgrat: Palästina
> Aus einem einzigen Knochen: Jerusalem.   (GW, I, 334)

It was a symbol, the final crystallization of her longing for a state of being which transcended all opposites, and where her world which, in the words of Peter Hille, 'had fallen apart' would become whole again. That no other place but Jerusalem could fulfil this symbolic function for her points at the passionate concern she felt for the Jews and their destiny – a love which included also the Jew Jesus Christ – and at the never-ending search for God in which this concern found its most intense expression.

C. Küster-Ginsberg has given a vivid description of the life of Else Lasker-Schüler in Jerusalem in an article she wrote in 1948 for *Blick in die Welt*,[1] a description which she has since elaborated for me in many personal talks. Else Lasker-Schüler was for most people only 'eine stadtbekannte komische verhutzelte Frau . . . die oft genug unmanierliche Kinder und unfreundliche Erwachsene auf der Straße zurechtwies', and only very few recognized in her the deeply original poet, perhaps

[1] Küster, *op. cit.*

34

the greatest poet the Jews have ever had. Some friends succeeded in securing a modest monthly income for her, and she spent her life in an unheated furnished room, where she did her own cooking and washing, harassed by a landlady who – without any feeling or understanding for her lodger – forced her to clean her room herself. This the more than seventy-year-old poet also managed to make bearable for herself by turning it into a game:

> Eines Tages kam sie auf die Idee, sich turnerische Übungen zu machen und dabei gleichzeitig das Zimmer zu reinigen. 'Jetzt weiß ich, wie man's macht, is' herrlich wie Schlittschuhlaufen!' Sie band sich Lappen um die Füße, tauchte sie in Petroleum, und reinigte damit auf dem Boden entlanggleitend ihr Zimmer. Sie tat es so lange, bis ihre Haut erkrankte.

She slept for many years in an easy-chair because she did not possess a bed, and did not want one either:

> 'Denkt daran, wie die Soldaten auf der Erde schlafen' war ihre Antwort, wenn die Freunde zu sehr drängten. Meistens aber sagte sie nur: 'Ihr solltet da mal schlafen, is' wie auf einer Schaukel und warm.' Als ihre Decke, vom Alter zermürbt, anfing zu zerfallen, stickte sie auf die Löcher Blumen aus bunter Wolle. Sie waren die einzigen in ihrem Zimmer.

She did not wish to leave this room 'weil es mitten im Leben lag', and because she could see from it 'über die Gräber auf die Berge Moabs'.

C. Küster-Ginsberg tells how difficult it was to help the poet who constantly bought little presents for her friends – flowers, chocolate and cheap jewellery – but was not prepared to accept anything herself: 'Wißt ihr denn nicht, daß ich zu arm bin zu nehmen?'

In January 1945, Else Lasker-Schüler had a severe heart-attack in the street; she collapsed and was brought to the Hadassa, the hospital on the Mount of Olives. About her death, a friend reports in a letter dated 23 January, the date of her funeral (K. in this letter is C. Küster-Ginsberg):

> Sie hat entsetzlich gelitten. Das Herz wollte nicht nachgeben . . .
> Erst am Montag um 5 Uhr morgens wurde die Atmung ruhiger . . .

Um 7 Uhr 25 morgens hauchte sie buchstäblich ihr Leben aus, sehr leise, ohne Kampf und in großer Ruhe . . . Als sie starb, war ich als einziger bei ihr. K. hatte vorher die ganzen Tage bei ihr zugebracht und ihr, soweit es möglich war, geholfen . . . Die Beerdigung war so würdig, wie es zu erwarten war. Ungefähr sechzig Leute erwiesen ihr, was man so die letzte Ehre nennt. Der Rabbiner Wilhelm sprach ihr Gedicht 'Ich weiß' aus dem blauen Klavier . . . K. legte als einzige auf ihr Grab wenige schöne Blumen. Und dann gingen alle zur Tagesordnung über.

(DD, pp. 599–60)

The Rabbi made a good choice in reading her poem *Ich weiß daß ich bald sterben muß* at her grave. All her life she had been preoccupied with the idea of death. But Gottfried Benn's suggestion for an epitaph[1] was perhaps even more appropriate. The four lines from her poem *An Gott* which he proposed as an inscription on her tombstone convey something of the suffering she endured in the struggle to reconcile the opposing forces outside and inside herself.

> Du wehrst den guten und den bösen Sternen nicht;
> Alle ihre Launen strömen.
> In meiner Stirne schmerzt die Furche,
> Die tiefe Krone mit dem düsteren Licht.   (GW, I, 171)

[1] Benn, *op. cit.* p. 540.

3. THE SWING OF THE PENDULUM

It is my intention to show the bipolar structure of Else Lasker-Schüler's mode of being, as it manifests itself in her poetry. I have chosen to start with an examination of the various manifestations of her tendency to withdraw from reality, and to follow this with a consideration of the opposite tendency, her outgoing search for contact.

This order of examination is not immediately given by the bipolar structure of withdrawal and outgoing. Using the image of the swinging pendulum, it is clear that, to some extent, it is arbitrary at what point we start to describe its movement. Throughout Else Lasker-Schüler's life, outgoing and withdrawal impulses alternated, often in quick succession. If, nevertheless, I have chosen to examine her search for contact *after* her tendency to withdraw, it is because I believe that in the highest manifestation of this search, her search for God, she came closest to reconciling the opposing forces, and that she came increasingly closer to this point of reconciliation – the point where the pendulum comes to rest in a centre – as she grew older.

The constant alternation of outgoing and withdrawal impulses is also reflected in her poetry. This fact poses a special problem in the development of my theme: for I find myself under the necessity of having to consider apart what, in reality, belongs together. In most of her poems outgoing and withdrawal elements can be found side by side, though emphasis may lie on one or the other. Similarly, the various forms of withdrawal shade into each other: thus, disappointment, resentment, despair, isolation and fantasies cannot always be clearly separated. In the same way, the longing for human contact, for the more specific erotic encounter and the search for God tend to merge. I have, nevertheless, attempted to find a number of poems which show a particular tendency sufficiently strongly to serve as illustrations, and I have added stanzas, or lines from other poems, for further elucidation.

37

Another difficulty must here be mentioned. An outgoing element can be coloured or distorted by an underlying withdrawal impulse, and vice versa; thus, the image of God can take on an infantile shape, while a concern with death will appear, at times, not as the extreme of self-destructiveness, but as a transition pointing towards acceptance and reconciliation. We are here faced with the basic problem which a necessarily 'linear' treatment of a 'polyphonic' theme presents: the limitations of any classification must constantly be borne in mind lest it turn into a straitjacket for the living phenomena which we are trying to observe.

Finally, I wish to say something about the way in which I have subdivided the two main parts of my work. The principle which I adopted in order to describe the various forms of withdrawal and outgoing we meet in Else Lasker-Schüler's poetry is that of intensification. Thus, in the section on withdrawal, disappointment is the awareness of a failure of contact, to which resentment is the aggressive reaction. Despair enlarges the area of resentment, turning it against the world as well as against oneself, while isolation is the resulting state of lack of contact. From this state, escape is sought in wishes for loss of life (concern with death) or loss of identity (flight into fantasies).

Similarly, the categories of outgoing present an intensification of the outgoing impulse: from the longing for contact in general through the specific wish for contact with another person in the erotic encounter to the search for the highest 'person', God.

(A) THE BACKWARD MOVEMENT: WITHDRAWAL

(1) *Disappointment and Resentment*

Abschied

Aber du kamst nie mit dem Abend –
Ich saß im Sternenmantel.

. . . Wenn es an mein Haus pochte,
War es mein eigenes Herz.

> Das hängt nun an jedem Türpfosten,
> Auch an deiner Tür;
>
> Zwischen Farren verlöschende Feuerrose
> Im Braun der Guirlande.
>
> Ich färbte dir den Himmel brombeer
> Mit meinem Herzblut.
>
> Aber du kamst nie mit dem Abend –
> . . . Ich stand in goldenen Schuhen.   (GW, I, 234)

The poem *Abschied* is found in the collection *Meine Wunder* and is included in the section dedicated to Hans Adalbert von Maltzahn. It is, therefore, possible that the poem is addressed to him, though love poems explicitly addressed to other men are included in this section. The factual circumstances under which Else Lasker-Schüler's poems were written are often very difficult, if not impossible, to ascertain. What matters here is that this is one of the numerous poems expressing her disappointment in someone's failure to return her love: the mere number of such poems indicates that the involvement was more often imaginary than actual.

The first and last stanzas describe the situation of disappointment: she was ready for the beloved, he did not come. Her readiness is expressed by the way in which she has adorned herself for him: 'Ich saß im Sternenmantel.' . . . 'Ich stand in goldenen Schuhen.'

In 'Sternenmantel' we meet one of Else Lasker-Schüler's most important, though also most elusive, symbols. In the context of this poem, 'Stern' probably signified, in Muschg's words, 'das Wunder schlechthin, die Gnade der Liebe'.[1] But Muschg proceeds to enumerate many other meanings, and we will come to see that the star is perhaps best understood as a symbol of transcendence.

She uses colour symbolically, as it was used by most German Expressionist writers and painters, particularly by her friend Franz Marc. Once more, we can follow Muschg, who suggests that 'das mythische Bild des Goldes' expresses in this poet's

---

[1] Muschg, *op. cit.* p. 142.

work 'vor allem die erotische Erfüllung'. (Guder's[1] interpretation of the colour gold as either indicating nobility or being just used for decoration seems to me insufficient.) Muschg adds that 'die Goldfarbe erzeugt bei ihr unfehlbar Märchenstimmung', and certainly a legendary feeling is created in this poem that removes the event from reality.

The second stanza depicts the sensation of futile waiting simply and realistically, but this is followed, in the following stanzas, by a sudden switch-over to fantastic elaboration, reminding one of the 'conceits' of seventeenth-century poetry. The heart is another fundamental symbol of Else Lasker-Schüler's, a 'Grundwort', as Muschg calls it.[2] Her use of it is essentially straightforward and traditional: it is the seat of feeling, and therefore, at the same time, the core of being. This basic meaning undergoes, however, a great many variations. The third stanza shows the heart exposed in all its vulnerability, and there is a characteristic tendency to turn the personal into the universal ('an jedem Türpfosten'). The fourth, with a sudden change of imagery, introduces the death theme, never far away in these poems of 'withdrawal': the heart has become a 'verlöschende Feuerrose'. In the fifth stanza, the depth of her love is expressed by a hyperbolic image which, again, is significant for her need to draw the whole world, here the sky, into the whirl of her feeling. This refusal to distinguish between objective reality and subjective experience, this 'romantische Ichbezogenheit' (Muschg),[3] is a fundamental aspect of Else Lasker-Schüler's life, as the outline of her biography has shown, and we meet it here as an important element in her poetry.

The emphasis in this poem is on the poet's disappointment in a love situation. No open resentment against the lover is expressed, though a faint note of reproach can perhaps be felt throughout which becomes audible in 'auch an deiner Tür' and 'Ich färbte dir den Himmel brombeer'. Such restraint is rare. In the following poem which belongs to the same collection, and

---

[1] G. Guder, *Else Lasker-Schüler*, Siegen, 1966, pp. 65–6.
[2] Muschg, *op. cit.* p. 141. [3] *Ibid.* pp. 123–4.

forms part of a cycle reflecting her relationship with Gottfried Benn, her resentment of the lover's rejection breaks through:

Hinter Bäumen berg ich mich

Bis meine Augen ausgeregnet haben,
Und halte sie tief verschlossen,
Daß niemand dein Bild schaut.

Ich schlang meine Arme um dich
Wie Gerank.

Bin doch mit dir verwachsen,
Warum reißt du mich von dir?

Ich schenkte dir die Blüte
Meines Leibes,

Alle meine Schmetterlinge
Scheuchte ich in deinen Garten.

Immer ging ich durch Granaten,
Sah durch dein Blut

Die Welt überall brennen
Vor Liebe.

Nun aber schlage ich mit meiner Stirn
Meine Tempelwände düster.

O du falscher Gaukler,
Du spanntest ein loses Seil.

Wie kalt mir alle Grüße sind,
Mein Herz liegt bloß,

Mein rot Fahrzeug
pocht grausig.

Bin immer auf See
Und lande nicht mehr.   (GW, I, 210–11)

The title of this poem which forms, at the same time, the first line states the theme of withdrawal: her reaction to her lover's rejection is to hide herself, and a state of isolation is already implied in this. (It can here be seen how impossible it is to separate the various 'categories' of withdrawal.) The next lines develop her conception of love as a complete fusion of the lovers, a conception which carries the seed of disappointment in itself: she has taken the image of the beloved, preserved in her

41

eyes, with her into hiding, guarding it jealously (stanzas 1 and 2) – as they had grown into one ('bin doch mit dir verwachsen'), how did he dare to destroy this one-ness (stanzas 3 and 4)? At this point, her resentment breaks into the open. It is interesting to see how clearly, though probably unintentionally, she expresses the suffocating effect which her total demand must have had on those she loved: 'Ich schlang meine Arme um dich / Wie Gerank.' It was this aspect of her approach to others which alienated many of her friends, and provoked the attacks of her enemies.

The next four stanzas further elaborate her vision of love: she has given herself totally, and has seen the whole world in terms of this fusion ('durch dein Blut'). Again, the equation between the world and herself is more than a metaphor: it is an expression of her way of being. In the lover's refusal the whole world seems to deny her. Stanzas 9 and 11–13 depict the poet's 'world' after the lover's refusal. Stanza 9 is elliptical; I suggest this paraphrase: her love has now become a prison, darkened by her self-destructive protest. The last three stanzas show in greater details the effect the lover's rejection has had on the poet's 'world'. All(!) greetings have become cold (stanza 11). Her heart, the vehicle that conveys her through life, is damaged and no longer able to bring her back to safety (stanzas 12 and 13). In these lines themes that go beyond disappointment and resentment are sounded: the image of the injured heart implies a threat to life itself, and the concluding lines conjure up the Flying Dutchman, a potent symbol of isolation.

This depiction of the way in which the poet's 'world' is affected by her disappointment is interrupted by two lines (stanza 10) which are a vehement expression of her resentment, taking the form of an accusation: the lover has tricked her. The image of the betrayer luring his victim on to a loose rope points at another aspect of Else Lasker-Schüler's view of her love relationships: she sees herself completely at the mercy of the other, balanced in a state of utter precariousness.

It is thus her own heart whose vulnerability she describes in a

variety of images, while the heart of the lover, in its stony coldness, represents the threat:

> Ich baute uns ein Himmelreich, dir unantastbar zu gehören
> – Das an den Riffen deiner Herzensnacht zerbrach.   (GW, I, 352)

> Als an deinem steinernen Herzen
> Meine Flügel brachen,
>
> Fielen die Amseln wie Trauerrosen
> Hoch vom blauen Gebüsch.   (GW, I, 245)

But the longing for the erotic encounter is only a particular
instance of her longing for contact; and disappointment and
resentment are experienced and expressed equally strongly on a
more general plane. In the early poem *Mein Drama*, there is a
sudden transition from the expression of frustration in a private
love situation to a total rejection of 'Mann und Weib':

> . . . Mit allen duftsüssen Scharlachblumen
> Hat er mich gelockt,
> Es regt sich wieder weh in meiner Seele
> Und leitet mich durch all' Erinnern weit.
> Sei still, mein wilder Engel mein,
> Gott weine nicht
> Und schweige von dem Leid,
> Mein Schmerzen soll sich nicht entladen,
> Keinen Glauben hab' ich mehr an Weib und Mann,
> Den Faden, der mich hielt mit allem Leben,
> Hab' ich der Welt zurückgegeben
> Freiwillig!   (GW, I, 44)

This rejection leads again to a withdrawal from 'allem Leben',
a withdrawal which gives the title to another early poem,
Weltflucht, which I wish to examine more closely:

> Ich will in das Grenzenlose
> Zu mir zurück,
> Schon blüht die Herbstzeitlose
> Meiner Seele,
> Vielleicht – ist's schon zu spät zurück!
> O, ich sterbe unter Euch!
> Da Ihr mich erstickt mit Euch.

Fäden möchte ich um mich ziehn –
Wirrwarr endend!
Beirrend,
Euch verwirrend,
Um zu entfliehn
Meinwärts!   (GW, I, 14)

Though this poem is not divided into stanzas, three parts can be clearly distinguished. The first (lines 1–5) expresses the wish to withdraw, the second (lines 6 and 7) says something about what provokes this withdrawal, the third (lines 8–13) elaborates the form which the withdrawal takes.

The first five lines work out the theme stated by the title: the poet wishes to withdraw 'in das Grenzenlose / Zu mir zurück' – the form of the escape from reality is that of a withdrawal to herself and beyond that into an undifferentiated realm which, I think, we would be justified in calling the unconscious. The use of another Freudian term seems equally appropriate, that of 'regression': the meeting with others is felt as too difficult, and a retreat into a more self-related ('narcissistic'), less conscious position is the result. The anxiety which such a situation generates is expressed in lines 3–5 where the 'autumn crocus of the soul' hints at the closeness of winter which here is probably an allusion to death. 'Vielleicht – ist's schon zu spät zurück!' is the voice of naked panic.

The next two lines give strong expression to the poet's resentment: other people are felt as a threat to her life, they suffocate her, it seems, by their very existence; no concrete reason is given. We meet such apparently unmotivated outbursts against 'die Menschen' also in her letters to Kraus; thus, she writes in a letter dated 20.4.11: 'Aber die Menschen sind mir über; ich bin müde' (BK, p. 44). Perhaps the occurrence of the word 'Wirrwarr' in line 9 throws some light on the nature of her feeling of suffocation: being with others inevitably causes 'confusion', reality is muddled and lacks the clear-cut, simple outlines of her image of paradise, and this 'confusion' can only be ended by separation.

The remainder of the poem shows how this separation comes about: the poet spins a web in order to cover her retreat 'meinwärts'. Heselhaus' comments on these lines are relevant:

> Dahinter steht das alte Dichter-Emblem: der Seidenwurm, der sich mit dem eigenen Gespinst sein Grab spinnt. Goethe hat dieses Bild, das schon bei Petrarca auftaucht, seinem Tasso in den Mund gelegt.[1]

In this poem, resentment of the others' existence is expressed without any disappointment being brought out. In the long poem *Mein stilles Lied* her disappointment in men as well as her desperate need for contact are displayed:

> Meine Lieder trugen des Sommers Bläue
> Und kehrten düster heim.
>
> Verhöhnt habt ihr mir meine Lippe
> Und redet mit ihr.
>
> Doch ich griff nach euren Händen,
> Denn meine Liebe ist ein Kind und wollte spielen.
>
> (GW, I, 134)

Here it is the rejection of her poetry, in which she quite naively saw a gift to the world, which throws her into disillusionment. The second of the three stanzas quoted here is rather enigmatic: what does 'Und redet mit ihr' mean? Perhaps an answer can be found in a sentence from a letter addressed to Kraus: '(. . .) aber alle lieben wohl meine Gedichte – Niemand mein Herz' (BK, p. 74). It seems to me as if the two lines in *Mein stilles Lied* echo this – a complaint that people try to dissociate her from her work, appreciating the poetry without acknowledging the poet.

Also the third stanza quoted here is worth looking at: it brings in two more key-words of Else Lasker-Schüler – 'Kind' and 'spielen'. Childhood meant to her a kind of paradise before the Fall, a return to it a way out of the 'Wirrwarr' of adult life. We shall have to concern ourselves with this aspect of her impulse to withdraw when we turn to her flight into fantasies. At this point, it seems to me important to observe that the image of

---

[1] Heselhaus, *op. cit.* p. 221.

love as a child arises at the very moment when she most passionately expresses her longing for contact. But where a grown-up
person's love wants to 'play', disappointment is inevitable. The
outgoing impulse is distorted by a regressive tendency.

Sometimes, the resentment of the other is balanced by a feeling
of her own failure. Thus, in *Abschied*, she says: 'Ich hab' die
Welt, die Welt hat mich betrogen' (GW, I, 318), and similarly
in *Dämmerung*, a poem published posthumously: 'Mich hat das
Leben, ich hab es verstoßen' (GW, III, 110). Something of a
realization of her own withdrawal from life which is seen as a
betrayal and a rejection breaks through. In *Abschied* this is
followed by a question which will be seen to be her principal
question: where, in all this, is God? Has he withdrawn from his
creature in anger and dismay?

> Warum hat Gott im Osten wetterleuchtend sich verzogen,
> Vom Ebenbilde Seines Menschen übermannt? (GW, I, 318)

The question remains here unanswered, and the poem ends on a
note of desolation:

> Und was mich je mit Seiner Schöpfung Ruhetag verband,
> Ist wie ein spätes Adlerheer unstät in diese Dunkelheit geflogen.
> (*ibid.*)

In *Dämmerung* the recognition of her own rejection of life is
followed by what seems to be a half-awareness of the precariousness of her flight into fantasy:

> Und lebe angstvoll nun im Übergroßen
> Im irdischen Leibe schon im Himmelreich.
> (GW, III, 110)

The withdrawal to an imaginary paradise, which is here seen as
a state of life-in-death, is experienced as 'angstvoll'.

In *Letzter Abend im Jahr*, she is able to express loneliness
without resentment:

> Mein Herz blieb ganz für sich
> Und fand auf Erden keinen Trost. (GW, I, 317)

The tone of this poem is one of sadness rather than anger, and out of this more accepting mood, a different kind of question arises, a question not about, but to, God:

> O Gott, wie kann der Mensch verstehen,
> Warum der Mensch haltlos vom Menschtum bricht,
> Sich wieder sammeln muß im höheren Geschehen.
>
> (GW, I, 317)

Another stage of her experience of loneliness is reached: she does not fight it, nor does she put all the blame on the behaviour of others – she simply asks for the ability to understand the limitations of man.

In her love poetry, too, she achieves at times a quieter, more accepting note, particularly in the cycle *An Ihn* which appeared two years before her death as the last section of her last collection of poetry. Here contact with the beloved remains unattainable, but resentment has given way to longing. The following poem conveys the theme of rejection with a quiet simplicity which she did not often command. Once again, the heart is the central symbol, but the imagery is here much less baroque:

> ### Und
>
> Und hast mein Herz verschmäht –
> In die Himmel wärs geschwebt
> Selig aus dem engen Zimmer!
>
> Wenn der Mond spazieren geht,
> Hör ichs pochen immer
> Oft bis spät.
>
> Aus Silberfäden zart gedreht
> Mein weiß Gerät –
> Trüb nun sein Schimmer. (GW, I, 359)

In the same cycle, however, we find also more discordant poems. In *Apollo* a number of different modes of reaction can be found side by side. There is the element of acceptance:

> Ich halte meine Hände still ergeben
> Auf meinem frommbezwungenen Schoß (GW, I, 369)

47

but also the escape into fantasy and the past:

> Ein Engel spielte sanft auf blauen Tasten,
> Langher verklungene Phantasie.   (*ibid.*)

There is the extravagantly phrased outburst of despair:

> Jäh tut mein sehr verwaistes Herz mir weh –
> Blutige Fäden spalten seine Stille.
> Zwei Augen blicken wund durch ihre Marmorhülle
> In meines pochenden Granates See.   (*ibid.*)

And there is the note of resentment against the unfaithful lover, characteristically transformed into the God Apollo:

> Nicht mal sein Götterlächeln
> Ließ er mir zum Pfande.   (*ibid.*)

Even at the end of her life, when she often came much closer to acceptance and reconciliation, the split was never quite healed.

(2) *Despair and Isolation*

Ich liege wo am Wegrand

> Ich liege wo am Wegrand übermattet –
> Und über mir die finstere kalte Nacht –
> Und zähl schon zu den Toten längst bestattet.
>
> Wo soll ich auch noch hin – von Grauen überschattet –
> Die ich vom Monde euch mit Liedern still bedacht
> Und weite Himmel blauvertausendfacht.
>
> Die heilige Liebe, die ihr blind zertratet,
> Ist Gottes Ebenbild . . . !
> Fahrlässig umgebracht.
>
> Darum auch lebten du und ich in einem Schacht!
> Und – doch im Paradiese trunken blumumblattet.
>
> (GW, I, 346)

With this text we move one step further on the path of withdrawal – from disappointment and resentment to despair and isolation. The first stanza of the poem conjures up the image of the aimless wanderer, a symbol of isolation like that of the never-landing sailor which we met earlier (see above, pp. 41–2). Night, as often in Else Lasker-Schüler's poetry, is experienced as cold and hostile, and the third line introduces the death-in-life theme to be examined at a later point. The next stanza elaborates the picture of the outcast: there is an element of resentment against those to whom she has given her songs and who have not accepted her, reminding us of the lines from *Mein stilles Lied* which we examined in the previous section (see above, p. 45):

> Meine Lieder trugen des Sommers Bläue
> Und kehrten düster heim.
>
> Verhöhnt habt ihr mir meine Lippe
> Und redet mit ihr.   (GW, I, 134)

In the corresponding lines 'Die ich vom Monde euch mit Liedern still bedacht / Und weite Himmel blauvertausendfacht' there is a note of superiority which can be found also in other poems, as for instance in *Ankunft*, another poem depicting extreme isolation, which ends with the line 'Aber meine Schultern heben sich, hochmütige Kuppeln'. By this superiority the outcast seems to take a revenge on a world that has rejected her, a revenge which in Else Lasker-Schüler's case we can assume to have been unconscious.

In this stanza we also meet an important example of Else Lasker-Schüler's colour symbolism. In her essay on Carl Sonnenschein, she herself commented on what some of the primary colours meant to her:

> Seine Seele, eine fromme dreifarbige Fahne; ihr weißes Linnen, ein Symbol seines makellosen Wandels, der rote Streif hielt sein Leben wach und lebendig für den aufopfernden Dienst an der Menschheit; doch das zarte Blau führte ihn ungehemmt in die höhere Welt.   (GW, II, 724)

It is this meaning of the colour blue that is carried by her neologism 'blauvertausendfacht'. Blue is for her the colour of the spirit, as it had been for the Middle Ages, not always simply 'Gottesfarbe', 'die Farbe der göttlichen Offenbarung',[1] but always pointing beyond the conflicts and confusion of worldly

---

[1] K. Lipfert, *Symbol-Fibel*, Kassel, 1956, p. 74.

existence, like the star a transcending symbol. In this poem, she sees herself as a kind of divine messenger, and this gives special weight to the world's rejection.

The accusation becomes more vehement in the following stanza: the world has not only refused the divine message, it has killed love itself, and as love is 'Gottes Ebenbild', it has killed God. Here is one of the approximations to Christian ideas to which we shall return. The consequences of the world's murder of love (=God) are expressed in the first line of the last stanza, and again we observe that romantic fusion of the universal and the personal characteristic of this poet: because 'ihr' (i.e. the world) have destroyed love, 'du und ich' (i.e. the poet and her lover) are imprisoned in darkness, 'in einem Schacht'.

The last line brings a sudden break-through of the opposite: the dark pit is also paradise. However, I am not certain whether this line expresses a genuine acceptance of the reality of human love, which, whatever its limitations, can still be 'blumumblattet', or whether the use of the word 'trunken' indicates a state less real and closer to a fantasy which drowns despair in forgetfulness.

The image of the eternal wanderer which dominates this poem recurs throughout Else Lasker-Schüler's poetry. Thus, *Lied meines Lebens* starts with the (twice-repeated) line 'Sieh in mein verwandertes Gesicht' (GW, I, 287), and one of the poems published in *Nachlaß* brings another variation on the theme of the sailor 'immer auf See':

> Wir treiben durch den Ozean der Luft,
> Und jedem Wind weiht jede Blume ihren Duft,
> Und immer landet nur der Tod (...)   (GW, III, 118)

In *Mein Tanzlied* the eternal dancer joins the eternal wanderer and the eternal sailor as an incarnation of rest- and rootlessness:

> So tanz' ich schon seit tausend Jahr,
> Seit meiner ersten Ewigkeiten.   (GW   66)

Despair is here experienced as an infinite state, as also in the poem that takes as its title and theme a line in which Richard Dehmel is said to have summed up his impression of the poet, 'Täubchen, das in seinem eigenen Blute schwimmt':

> Als ich also diese Worte an mich las,
> Erinnerte ich mich
> Tausend Jahre meiner.
>
> Eisige Zeiten verschollen – Leben vom Leben,
> Wo liegt mein Leben –
> Und träumt nach meinem Leben.
>
> Ich lag allen Tälern im Schoß,
> Umklammerte alle Berge,
> Aber nie meine Seele wärmte mich (. . .)   (GW, I, 119)

This experience of being 'verschollen' we found condensed into the two words 'wurde Robinson' in the biographical sketch which she wrote for *Menschheitsdämmerung* (see above, p. 15). In one of her essays, after remembering a family scene which spelt warmth and security, she writes:

> Das ist lange her, ich weiß auch nicht, warum ich daran so oft denke, zumal ich doch Robinson wurde, durchbrannte in die Welt, weil ich dem Robinson auf dem Deckel seiner Geschichte so ähnlich sah.   (GW, II, 179)

But there was also the fear of the crippling narrowness of such security, hinted at in the next sentence of this passage:

> Und ich liebte das Abenteuer, das hat nichts mit der Stube zu tun, und wenn es auch eine herrliche ist.   (*ibid.*)

In a letter to Ludwig von Ficker, the editor of *Der Brenner* and friend of Trakl, this longing for the sea as an embodiment of creative freedom, and the dread of the inhibiting heaviness of 'das Schwarze der Erde', finds vivid expression:

> Lauter Wasser, manchmal hängen Muscheln an mir, Seetiere; ich erschrecke nur, wenn Erde an mir hängt. Ich finde das Schwarze der Erde nicht abzuschütteln. Ich bin so herunter, sitz ich und will dichten, bin ich wie Welle, muß zurück, so aber ohne Strand und Hand.[1]

[1] W. von Schneditz, *Trakl in Zeugnissen der Freunde*, Salzburg, 1951, p. 89.

The last sentence points to the ambiguity of her experience: she feels the threat of 'Erde', of security; but the insecurity of 'lauter Wasser', of being 'ohne Strand', leaves her also 'ohne Hand', that is paralysed, without creative impulse.

In *Ich liege wo am Wegrand* we find the elements of disappointment and resentment intensified to despair and isolation. But there is still a reference to a specific love relationship. The following poem conveys the state of despair as such, in all its nakedness:

Chaos

Die Sterne fliehen schreckensbleich
Vom Himmel meiner Einsamkeit,
Und das schwarze Auge der Mitternacht
Starrt näher und näher.

Ich finde mich nicht wieder
In dieser Todverlassenheit!
Mir ist: ich lieg' von mir weltenweit
Zwischen grauer Nacht der Urangst . . .

Ich wollte, ein Schmerzen rege sich
Und stürze mich grausam nieder
Und riß mich jäh an mich!
Und es lege eine Schöpferlust
Mich wieder in meine Heimat
Unter der Mutterbrust.

Meine Mutterheimat ist seeleleer,
Es blühen dort keine Rosen
Im warmen Odem mehr. –
. . . Möcht einen Herzallerliebsten haben!
Und mich in seinem Fleisch vergraben.   (GW, I, 39)

As so often, the first stanza presents the theme as an image. The stars, symbols of the grace of love, are in flight from what she calls, with characteristic ambiguity, the 'Himmel meiner Einsamkeit'. Again, night is experienced as a threat. In the next stanza, the poet describes a state of extreme abandonment: this is felt in the first two lines, once more, as 'Todverlassenheit', in the following two as an estrangement from herself in 'grauer Nacht der Urangst'. It is interesting to observe how here, as in other places, the extreme emotional pressure destroys the grammatical structure: 'zwischen' is, of course, grammatically incorrect here, but it conveys the feeling of being caught more precisely than any other preposition.

The beginning of the third stanza shows her intuitive psychological awareness: if only she could feel pain, she would come to herself again. The deadness which is at the core of despair is this very inability to feel the pain that is nevertheless there, though cut off from conscious experience. The poet's intuition expresses a truth which is the psychotherapist's daily experience. In these lines there is an opening towards reality from which, however, she turns away in the remainder of the stanza: there is a regressive movement towards childhood, towards the 'Heimat unter der Mutterbrust'.

The impossibility of such a 'return' is seen at the beginning of the last stanza, but in regret, not in acceptance. The end of the poem brings the image of sexual union as an alternative out of the 'chaos' of despair. But this is seen as a means to forget, a kind of death ('Und mich in seinem Fleisch vergraben') rather than a forward movement towards contact and meeting.

All concrete references have disappeared from this poem. A fundamental state of mind is revealed which is perhaps best understood through the keyword 'Urangst'. Anxiety is the emotional experience which, above all, characterizes the state of rootlessness and isolation. F. J. Schneider points to Else Lasker-Schüler's great gift for expressing this experience:

> Kein Moderner hat ergreifender wie sie die beklemmenden Angstgefühle eines einsam, steuer- und kompasslos gewordenen Menschenherzen ausgesprochen.[1]

The poet herself, in *Ich räume auf,* has linked the feeling of not belonging anywhere with the experience of 'Angst':

> (. . .) überall blicke ich nach einem heimatlichen Boden aus, wer von uns hätte den gefunden und nicht erlitten des Heimwehs qualvollste Angst. (GW, II, 534)

---

[1] F. J. Schneider, *Der expressive Mensch und die deutsche Lyrik der Gegenwart*, Stuttgart, 1927, p. 25.

Existentialist philosophy, taking its cue from Kierkegaard, has been particularly concerned with the analysis of 'Angst':

> Fragen wir uns näher, welches der Gegenstand der Angst ist, so ist hier allewege zu antworten: Dieser ist das Nichts. Die Angst und das Nichts entsprechen einander beständig.[1]

What she describes as 'chaos' in her poem comes very close to what the philosopher calls 'das Nichts' – a state of extreme isolation, without any contact, without anything to refer to beyond itself (– the stars, symbols of transcendence, have fled).

This experience need not end in negation. Kierkegaard also says:

> So ist die Angst der Schwindel der Freiheit. Sie entsteht, wenn die Freiheit . . . in ihre eigene Möglichkeit hinunterschaut . . .[2]

On this O. F. Bollnow, in his conspectus of existentialist philosophy, comments:

> . . . erst im Aushalten dieser letzten Verlassenheit entdeckt er [that is the person experiencing anxiety] seine wirkliche existentielle Freiheit.[3]

In another passage, Bollnow elaborates this:

> Die Angst ist notwendig, um den Menschen aus dem Gleichmaß seines alltäglichen, gedankenlosen Hinlebens aufzuscheuchen.[4]

The experience of 'existential anxiety' is always also an opportunity for change. It is the point where the pendulum may swing in the opposite direction. In this poem, as we have seen, this does not happen: in sexual and childhood fantasies the opportunity is lost.

But there are poems which show such a turning point. In such poems, questions again occur, carrying the poet's search for meaning. They are usually questions to God:

[1] S. Kierkegaard, *Der Begriff Angst*, Collected Works, v, Jena, 1922, p. 93.
[2] *Ibid.* p. 57.
[3] O. F. Bollnow, *Existenzphilosophie*, 5th ed., Stuttgart, 1960, p. 69.   [4] *Ibid.* p. 68.

Ich suchte Gott auf innerlichsten Wegen
Und kräuselte die Lippe nie zum Spott.
In meinem Herzen fällt ein Tränenregen;
Wie soll ich dich erkennen lieber Gott ... (GW, I, 315)

O mein Gott mein, nur alleine,
Ich verdurste und verweine
In dem Segen (. . .)

Und ich kann es nicht verstehen,
Da ich unter seinem Dach
Oft so traurig erwach. (GW, I, 323)

There are attempts to understand her despair as a kind of atonement for her neglect of the task which God has given her:

Es lehren Flügelmenschen, die des Wegs ein Stück
Mich, meines Amtes wegen, stärken und begießen –
Und wieder jenseits in die Lüfte fließen:
Daß ich für – unerfüllte Gottesweisung – büße. (GW, I, 348)

We have seen before how much she saw her writing of poetry as a divine 'office', and that she considered the rejection of her poems by the world as a rejection of something larger than herself. In this stanza she takes upon herself the responsibility which such an 'office' carries.

In *Aus der Ferne* she sees exile itself as a condition for a closer contact with God:

Es wachsen auch die Seelen der verpflanzten Bäume
Auf Erden schon in Gottes blaue Räume,
Um inniger von Seiner Herrlichkeit zu träumen. (GW, I, 328)

In this, as in many others of her poems, the appearance of God is like a break in the wall of isolation, the possibility of contact enters like a shaft of light, and despair turns into sadness and longing.

In these poems, the pendulum swings out of despair forward into a search for meaning – in *Ankunft*, by contrast, the pendulum, swinging back into complete withdrawal, has reached a point of isolation where despair is no longer felt:

Ich bin am Ziel meines Herzens angelangt.
Weiter führt kein Strahl.
Hinter mir laß ich die Welt,
Fliegen die Sterne auf: Goldene Vögel.

Hißt der Mondturm die Dunkelheit –
...O, wie mich leise eine süße Weise betönt ...
Aber meine Schultern heben sich, hochmütige Kuppeln.

(GW, I, 154)

Title and first line show to what extent the poet has here given in to the impulse of withdrawal: isolation is described as her destination, the 'Ziel meines Herzens'. The following line emphasizes this affirmation of a reversal of the forward movement: for a ray is usually imagined as radiating outwards rather than inwards. In the third line, the withdrawal from the world is unambiguously stated, and the last line of this stanza echoes the beginning of *Chaos*: the stars, symbols of a transcending love, are moving away.

The first line of the second stanza, in a bold metaphor, introduces once again night as a symbol of isolation, but this time not as a threat, but welcoming the poet's 'arrival' like a flag. The magic powers conjured up by 'Mondturm' become potent in the following line depicting the drug-like quality of this state of mind: we are reminded of the song of the Sirens. The poem ends, as we saw before (see above, p. 49), on a note of superiority characteristic for the illusionary happiness which a state of complete isolation can create.

One other way in which Else Lasker-Schüler expresses despair and isolation in her poetry remains to be considered – that of 'objectification'. Many, perhaps the majority, of her poems embody the inner reality of her state of mind in images which, for all their vividness, have little relation to the objective world around her. They are, predominantly, 'I-poems'.

But there came the moment when the outcast in mind became the outcast in fact: when she had to leave Germany as a refugee. Suddenly, inner and outer reality fused, and the shock was overwhelming. Thus she writes on 24 January 1933 to the late Professor William Rose:

Die furchtbaren Ereignisse erschreckten mich kürzlich so, daß ich ganz krank wurde, lag. Und ich schreibe liegend an Sie ...[1]

[1] Quoted from the original postcard in possession of the Institute of Germanic Studies, London.

The poem *Die Verscheuchte* (see above, p. 33), in which the experience and the suffering of sudden exile is crystallized, shows the poet's imagination anchored, as it were, in a concrete situation. Heselhaus, in his analysis of the poem,[1] compares it with *Weltflucht*, and rightly stresses its greater immediacy, its increased 'Naturanschauung'. He quotes a passage from a letter to Hulda Pankok in which she describes how she spent the first days in exile 'am See unter einem Baum versteckt' and links it with the line 'Ich streife heimatlos zusammen mit dem Wild'. But I suggest that it is the fact that the 'eternal wanderer' has ceased to be a metaphor and has become a deeply suffered reality which gives the poem its immediacy and keeps it free from the hyperbolic excesses found in some of her more 'subjective' poetry. When we compare

> Ich will in das Grenzenlose
> > Zu mir zurück,
> Schon blüht die Herbstzeitlose
> > Meiner Seele,
> Vielleicht – ist's schon zu spät zurück!   (GW, I, 14)

with

> Wo soll ich hin, wenn kalt der Nordsturm brüllt?
> Die scheuen Tiere aus der Landschaft wagen sich
> Und ich vor deine Tür, ein Bündel Wegerich.
>
> (GW, I, 347)

the gain in precision and poignancy is striking.

The poet herself refers to this correspondence between inner and outer exile in another letter to Professor Rose, written five years later (I quote the passage from the typewritten letter without change):

> I am so tired from all thinks in the World and from my live.
> 6 Years auf Wanderschaft allways, sir, also in heart I mean.

But she achieved an even greater degree of 'objectification' already twenty years before *Die Verscheuchte* was written. (Again, we see that no straight-line 'development' can be traced in this poet's work.) *Die Verscheuchte* remains an 'I-poem',

---

[1] Heselhaus, *op. cit.* pp. 221–2.

though the experience it expresses is rooted in objective fact. But in 1913 a collection of Else Lasker-Schüler's poetry appeared under the title of *Hebräische Balladen* which to a great extent consisted of re-interpretations of Old Testament events and where the 'I' of the poet has withdrawn behind the stories she interprets. The stories of Abel, Joseph, Moses, Saul and other biblical figures served as 'objective correlatives', to use T. S. Eliot's phrase, for the emotions which the poet wished to express. Thus, in the following poem the experience of separation, exile and despair is made concrete through the highly original re-telling of an ancient story:

Hagar und Ismael

Mit Muscheln spielten Abrahams kleine Söhne
Und ließen schwimmen die Perlmutterkähne;
Dann lehnte Isaak bang sich an den Ismael

Und traurig sangen die zwei schwarzen Schwäne
Um ihre bunte Welt ganz dunkle Töne,
Und die verstoßne Hagar raubte ihren Sohn sich schnell.

Vergoß in seine kleine ihre große Träne,
Und ihre Herzen rauschten wie der heilige Quell,
Und übereilten noch die Straußenhähne.

Die Sonne aber brannte auf die Wüste grell
Und Hagar und ihr Knäblein sanken in das gelbe Fell
Und bissen in den heißen Sand die weißen Negerzähne.

(GW, I, 295)

We meet here familiar themes: the vision of a childhood paradise, Isaac's and Ishmael's 'bunte Welt' which is 'blackened' by rejection and the breaking-up of relationship, and in consequence the painful departure into the 'desert' of desolation. We know these experiences to be very specifically Else Lasker-Schüler's own: but here she has distanced herself from them, is no longer identified with them, and through this has, I think, heightened their impact and the degree of their universal validity.

(3) *Escape into Fantasy*

(a) *Childhood; Lost Paradise*

In our biographical outline, we have met Else Lasker-Schüler's need to mythify her life, particularly to re-think and re-feel her childhood into a kind of paradise, inhabited by the legendary figures of father, mother and brother. This myth she created as a sanctuary for herself where she could feel safe from the 'Tatsächlichkeiten des empirischen Neben- und Nacheinander'.[1] Heinz Politzer's statement that 'Else Lasker-Schüler did not go back to her childhood or past, but to the myth, the prehistoric past'[2] is not quite correct: there are, in fact, many poems in which actual childhood figures and events are referred to, though they appear remoulded into images of myth. But there are also others in which the concrete past has been left behind, and only the 'feel' of childhood as a lost and ever-longed-for paradise is conveyed, as in *Im Anfang*:

> Hing an einer goldenen Lenzwolke,
> Als die Welt noch Kind war,
> Und Gott noch junger Vater war.
> Schaukelte, hei!
> Auf dem Ätherei,
> Und meine Wollhärchen flitterten ringelrei.
> Neckte den wackelnden Mondgroßpapa,
> Naschte Goldstaub der Sonnenmama,
> In den Himmel sperrte ich Satan ein
> Und Gott in die rauchende Hölle ein.
> Die drohten mit ihrem größten Finger
> Und haben 'klumbumm! klumbumm!' gemacht
> Und es sausten die Peitschenwinde!
> Doch Gott hat nachher zwei Donner gelacht
> Mit dem Teufel über meine Todsünde.
> Würde 10000 Erdglück geben,
> Noch einmal so gottgeboren zu leben,
> So gottgeborgen, so offenbar.
> Ja! Ja!
> Als ich noch Gottes Schlingel war!   (GW, I, 76)

[1] F. J. Schneider, *op. cit.* p. 25.   [2] H. Politzer, *op. cit.* p. 338.

59

This poem is the last in her first collection. It conjures up the vision of paradise seen through the eyes of a child, describes playfully (as the subtitle of its first version, 'Weltscherzo', which the poet later dropped, announces), almost in the manner of a nursery rhyme.

The poem has no strophic structure; but for the sake of analysis three sections can be distinguished. Lines 1–6 show the world 'in the beginning' with God as its 'young father', and the poet herself as a child in it, swinging on the 'there-egg' (from which the world, or herself, has hatched?), with her curly hair dancing a ring-a-ring-a-roses.

The central part describes the child's misbehaviour: she teases grandfather Moon, nibbles from grandmother Sun's gold-dust, and even locks Satan up in Heaven, and God in Hell – but this 'Todsünde' has no serious consequences: for this is a world entirely beyond Good and Evil.

The last five lines express the poet's longing for such a world: she is ready to give all earthly happiness for this state of 'Gottgeborgenheit' – for the idyllic security of being 'Gottes Schlingel'. This expression which might be translated, not quite precisely, as 'God's naughty boy' is something of a key-word. The longing for God is here expressed as a longing for irresponsibility, for a withdrawal into a world of playfulness and unreality. The image of God is carried by the backward swing of the pendulum into the realm of fairy-tale.

This longing for a time long ago when all was play and harmony is, of course, not only an individual experience, but is also met as a collective phenomenon in the Greek myth of the 'Golden Age' where people 'lived without cares or labour, eating only acorns, wild fruit, and honey that dripped from the trees ... never growing old, dancing and laughing much ...'.[1] Robert Graves's comments on this myth are of some interest in our context, though they do, in accordance with his exclusively historical approach, overlook the universality of the experience: he interprets the myth as an idealization of 'pre-agricultural times'

[1] Robert Graves, *Greek Myths*, London, 1958, p. 36.

whose 'savagery . . . had been forgotten by Hesiod's day'.[1] Her childhood also is unlikely to have been as idyllic as she makes it appear. When she writes to a twelve-year-old girl 'Und wie gefällt Dir die Schule? Ich saß nämlich immer untenan und lauter Tadel bekam ich eingeschrieben. Machs auch so!' (DD, p. 539), a less paradisical picture seems to emerge from between the lines, in spite of 'Machs auch so!'.

But on the whole, a view of childhood as an ideal state of being pervades her writing. 'Tatsächlich, ein anständiger Mensch hat sein lebenlang Primaner zu bleiben' (GW, II, 549), she exclaims in one of her essays, and the first paragraph of the prose poem which closes her last collection of poetry echoes the letter to her twelve-year-old friend, but with a romantic trans-figuration of the difficulties of school life:

> Ich sitze noch heute sitzengeblieben auf der untersten Bank der Schulklasse, wie einst . . . Doch mit spätem versunkenem Herzen: 1000 und 2-jährig, dem Märchen über den Kopf gewachsen.
>
> (GW, I, 371)

Werner Kraft, as a comment on her idealization of childhood (in which he, however, does not appear to see the latent danger), quotes a passage from Nietzsche's *Menschliches, Allzumensch-liches*:

> Er (d.i. der Künstler) ist zeitlebens ein Kind oder ein Jüngling geblieben und auf dem Standpunkt zurückgehalten, auf welchem er von seinem Kunsttriebe überfallen wurde; Empfindungen der ersten Lebensstufen stehen aber zugestandenermaßen denen früherer Zeitläufte näher als denen des gegenwärtigen Jahrhunderts. Unwillkürlich wird es zu seiner Aufgabe, die Menschheit zu verkind-lichen: dies ist sein Ruhm und seine Begrenztheit.[2]

We have, however, seen – in poems like *Chaos* and *Mein stilles Lied* (see above, pp. 52–3 and 45, 49) – how such a 'Verkindlichung' which inevitably contains elements of falsification often means a loss of contact and withdrawal from reality. It seems to me neces-sary to distinguish this from the capacity of keeping alive in oneself

---

[1] *Ibid.*   [2] Kraft, *op. cit.* p. 11.

the child's openness to experience which is, to some extent, a condition of creative activity and was certainly a quality Else Lasker-Schüler possessed in rich measure.

In some poems, childhood is presented very specifically as the state of innocence, a mode of being without sin, and growing up then appears as a kind of 'fall'. In *Der gefallene Engel*, the poet addresses her friend, the vagabond-poet Peter Hille, as 'St. Petrus Hille', and seeing in him the redeeming power of Christ ('Des Nazareners Lächeln strahlt aus deinen Mienen'), she asks for his help.

> Darf ich mit Dir auf weiten Höhen schreiten!
> Hand in Hand, Du und ich, wie Kinder . . .
> Wenn aus dem Abendhimmel wilde Sterne gleiten
> Durch's tiefe Blauschwarz, wie verstoss'ne Sünder,
> Und scheu in Gärten fallen, die voll Orchideen
> Und stummen Blüten steh'n
> In gold'nen Hüllen.
>
> Und in den Kronen schlanker Märchenbäume
> Harrt meine Unschuld unter Wolkenflor,
> Und meine ersten, holden Kinderträume
> Erwachen vor dem gold'nen Himmelsthor.
> Und wenn wir einst ins Land des Schweigens gehen,
> Der schönste Engel wird mein Heil erfleh'n
> Um Deiner Liebe willen.   (GW, I, 50)

The condition for 'salvation' is the re-awakening of the poet's 'ersten, holden Kinderträume'. Once more we meet the symbol of the stars, but here they have become 'wild', 'verstoß'ne Sünder', have fallen from grace. The state of sin is symbolized by gardens 'full of orchids' – probably an image of sexual involvement: we have already met the erotic connotation of the colour 'golden', and the orchid is a common sexual symbol. Other lines, occurring earlier in the poem, also suggest such an interpretation:

> (. . .) Und meine Lippen öffnen sich mit Zagen,
> Wie gift'ge Blüten, die dem Satan dienen (. . .)
>
> (. . .) Und meine Träume tränkt ein blut'ger Regen
> Und reizt mit seinem Schein zum Laster meine Nerven (. . .)

(. . .) Und diese roten, feurigen Granaten
Gab mir ein Königgreis für meine Nächte, (. . .)

(GW, I, 49)

From this poem, an image emerges of childhood as a paradise
which is lost through 'Satan's' sexual temptation, and can be
regained with the help of a child-like saint.

In *Hundstage*, the poet, in despair over the uncertain intentions
of her lover ('Von der Tollwut der Zweifel zerbissen'), again
recalls childhood as a time of peace and security.

... Wie friedvoll die Malvenblüten starben
Unter süssen Himmeln der Lenznacht –
Ich war noch ein Kind, als sie starben.

Hab' so still in der Seele Gottes geruht – (. . .) (GW, I, 68)

In some of her poems, her fantasy withdraws, so to speak,
behind and beyond childhood, into what we could rightly call,
with Politzer, a 'prehistoric past':

Es ist so dunkel heut am Heiligen Himmel . . .
Ich und die Abendwolken suchen nach dem Mond –
Wo beide wir einst vor dem Erdenleben,
Schon nahe seiner Leuchtewelt gewohnt.   (GW, I, 367)

Once, 'vor dem Erdenleben', the lovers were united. The
darkness of today is contrasted with the 'Leuchtewelt' of some
'prehistoric' existence.

This theme recurs, though with an essential difference, in
Ich schlafe in der Nacht, published after her death:

Ich schlafe in der Nacht an fremden Wänden
Und wache in der Frühe auf an fremder Wand.
Ich legte mein Geschick in harten Händen
Und reihe Tränen auf, so dunkle Perlen ich nie fand.

Ich habe einmal einen blauen Pfad gekannt
Doch weiß ich nicht mehr wo ich mich vor dieser Welt befand.
Und – meine Sehnsucht will nicht enden ! . . .

Vom Himmel her sind beide wir verwandt
Und unsere Seelen schweben übers Heilige Land
In *einem* Sternenkleide leuchtend um die Lenden.   (GW, III, 123)

The first stanza calls up, once more, the lonely, uprooted life of the outcast which at the time this poem was written was no doubt already a hard reality for the poet. In the second stanza, the poet's longing for 'einen blauen Pfad' reminds us of the German romantic's search for the 'blaue Blume'. But we have seen that for her the colour blue leads 'in die höhere Welt', that it indicates a transcendence of worldly confusion, and in thus hinting at a possibility of reconciliation, it points not only backwards but also forwards.

The last stanza of the poem brings this out: here the 'path' to union lies no longer in the past, 'vor dieser Welt' – the lovers' separation is overcome in the here-and-now, transcendence has become reality through reconciliation ('in *einem* Sternenkleide') and the lovers' union is itself a symbol of a more universal, transcendental state of being which appears here crystallized in the image of the 'Heilige Stadt', Jerusalem (see also pp. 34 and 149–51).

Mother

We have previously seen how great a part Else Lasker-Schüler's mother played in her life (see above, pp. 19–21). Sigrid Bauschinger has interpreted the meaning of this poet's work in terms of her relationship with mother ('Ein Kind sucht in diesem Werke nach der Mutter, im Bereich der Natur, im Wasser, in der Erde, unter den Bäumen, im Schutz der Nacht und im Schein der Sterne'),[1] and though such a monistic approach seems to me to sacrifice a wealth of phenomena to one single idea, the role of the mother as unrivalled queen of the poet's childhood paradise nevertheless deserves special consideration in our study.

In *Chaos* (see above, p. 52) we met her longing for a return to the infant's intimate relationship with mother in which alone she saw 'home' ('Ich wollte (. . .) / (. . .) es lege eine Schöpferlust / Mich wieder in meine Heimat / Unter der Mutterbrust'). The poem *Mutter*, written very much later, expresses the same longing.

[1] Bauschinger, *op. cit.* p. 146.

Mutter

O Mutter, wenn du leben würdest,
Dann möcht ich spielen in deinem Schoß.

Mir ist bang und mein Herz schmerzt
Von der vielen Pein.
Überall sprießt Blutlaub.

Wo soll mein Kind hin?
Ich baute keinen Pfad froh,
Alle Erde ist aufgewühlt.

Liebe, liebe Mutter.   (GW, I, 276)

This is a simple poem which needs little comment. 'Überall sprießt Blutlaub' is another example of the poet's tendency to turn private loss into cosmic catastrophe. The third stanza is important for the light it throws on her own experience of motherhood, by linking her inability to build a 'Pfad' for her son, to create a secure basis for his life, with her never-accepted loss of her own mother.

Sigrid Bauschinger rightly points to the fact that Else Lasker-Schüler does not seem to have written any poem 'das von der lebenden Mutter spricht',[1] and raises the question whether she did not perhaps only start writing after her mother's death. Against this, we have the poet's own statement: 'die Gedichte meines ersten Buches dichtete ich zwischen 15 und 17' (GW, II, 250). But we have also seen that at times she made herself seven years younger than she was. All this lies in the realm of speculation, but it is possible that the following poem, which appeared in her first collection, was written under the immediate impact of her mother's death:

Mutter

Ein weisser Stern singt ein Totenlied
     In der Julinacht,
Wie Sterbegeläut in der Julinacht.
Und auf dem Dach die Wolkenhand,
Die streifende, feuchte Schattenhand
Sucht nach meiner Mutter.
Ich fühle mein nacktes Leben,

---

[1] *Ibid.* p. 150.

Es stößt sich ab vom Mutterland,
So nackt war nie mein Leben,
So in die Zeit gegeben,
Als ob ich abgeblüht
Hinter des Tages Ende,
    Versunken
Zwischen weiten Nächten stände,
Von Einsamkeiten gefangen.
Ach Gott! Mein wildes Kindesweh!
. . . Meine Mutter ist heimgegangen.   (GW, I, 13)

The first six lines once more make the cosmos the carrier of the poet's private loss – it is the star that mourns, the cloud that searches for the dead mother. The impression here, however, is not so much one of romantic exaggeration as almost of objectification: the poet distances herself from her grief. But with the seventh line, the poet enters, so to speak, the poem with an image that expresses the ambiguity of the situation: for it indicates birth as well as deprivation. From the eleventh line on, however, there is nothing left but a feeling of utter desolation. 'Ich fühle mein nacktes Leben / Es stößt sich ab vom Mutterland' still means a new beginning, the need to live without the dominating influence of mother which, with all its painfulness, is yet an opportunity. But '(. . .) abgeblüht / Hinter des Tages Ende' seems to deny the possibility of any further life at all.

'Als ob ich (. . .) / (. . .) / Zwischen weiten Nächten stände' anticipates lines in *Chaos* which have been considered earlier: 'Mir ist: ich lieg' von mir weltenweit / Zwischen grauer Nacht der Urangst' (see above, p. 52): again, night becomes the symbol of extreme isolation. Sigrid Bauschinger's insistence that for Else Lasker-Schüler night is 'ihrer Natur nach das Bild der gütigen Mutter' with the qualification 'Überall wo sie nicht in dieser Gestalt erscheint, hat sie sich durch schreckliche Ereignisse gewandelt . . .'[1] shows, I think, again the limitations of the reductive approach which loses the weight of the actual phenomenon, here the experience of night as a desolate vastness in which the poet is utterly lost.

[1] *Ibid.* p. 79.

She omitted the last two lines in a later version of the poem (GW, I, 275), probably because she felt – rightly, I think – that in them raw emotion was insufficiently transformed into poetry. Whether the other change she made, the substitution of 'Alleine' for 'Von Einsamkeiten gefangen', is equally successful seems to me questionable.

There is yet another version of this poem, textually not different from the second (1917), but showing a division into four three-line stanzas, which appeared in her prose book *Das Hebräerland* as late as 1937. That it was possible for her to reprint this poem as part of a new work thirty-five years after it was first written, conveys something of her unchanged feeling throughout her life about her mother's death. In *Das Hebräerland* she also wrote:

> Eines Morgens neigte sich meine unvergeßliche Mutter über mich Erwachende und lächelte . . . Nach diesem Lächeln habe ich mich seit ihrem Heimgang zu Gott gesehnt. Es erwärmte und kräftigte mich als Kind schon, und seitdem ich dieses Wunderlächeln hier in Jerusalem erleben durfte, begann ich eine niegekannte Freude und ein tiefes Verständnis zum Heiligen Lande zu empfinden, zu unserem lieben Heiligen Lande. (GW, II, 961)

Throughout her life, she saw in her mother a kind of guiding spirit, a guardian angel:

> War sie der große Engel,
> Der neben mir ging? (GW, I, 169)

> Und weiß es nicht, ob meine Mutter mein . . .
> Es war, die mir erschien im lichten Engelkleid . . .
> (GW, I, 411)

> (. . .) Sterb ich am Wegrand wo, liebe Mutter, kommst du und
> trägst mich hinauf zum blauen Himmel. (GW, I, 371)

In the prose extract from *Das Hebräerland*, the awareness of her mother's presence leads to a deeper experience of Jerusalem; the image of her mother does not lure the poet back into the past, but helps to a 'niegekannte Freude und ein tiefes Verständnis' of

67   3-2

the Holy Land, here and now. On the other hand, in *Resignation*
which starts

> Umarm' mich mütterlich und weich,
> Und zeige mir das Himmelreich,
> Du träumerische Nacht; (. . .)

and ends

> Und sehne mich nach ew'ger Nacht.
> Zu schmelzen still im Abendrot,
> In deinem Heilandarme, Tod.   (GW, III, 135)

the 'motherly' arms of the night become the 'Heilandarm' of
death. Once more we see the point from where the pendulum
can swing in either direction.

Play

One important aspect of her nostalgic view of childhood is her
passionate 'Spiellust' which she felt she had inherited from her
father (see above, p. 19). Her poetry abounds with references to
'Spiel', 'spielen' and 'Spielsachen', and she repeatedly compared
the process of writing with that of playing:

> Ob man mit grünen, lila und blauen Steinen spielt oder ob man
> dichtet, das ist ganz dasselbe, man hat dasselbe Glücksgefühl
> denn bunter kann man die Welt auch nicht durch den Rausch
> als durch die Gläser sehen.   (BK, p. 11)

> Ich gebe mir Müh, aber ich kann nur spielen, auch in der
> Schreiberei.   (*ibid.* p. 57)

In another letter to Kraus, she defends her habit of turning her
friends into mythical figures and letting them appear in her books
(she thinks that Kraus has expressed himself critically about
this in a letter to Walden):

> Ich kann mir ja nur denken, daß Sie nicht gegen meine Dichtung
> etwa schrieben, [sondern] nur [dagegen] daß ich allerlei Figur
> mitspielen lasse. (. . .) Jedenfalls liebe ich nach meiner Sehnsucht
> die Leute alle zu kleiden, damit ein Spiel zu Stande kommt.
> (. . .) Spielen ist alles. Sie, Minister, der Sie am aller entzücktesten
> wären, würden Sie wirklich mal die Spiele erleben, die ich noch
> spielen könnte, beklagen sich über endlich, endlichen Frühling
> in der Dichtung.   (*ibid.* pp. 38–9)

Without entering too deeply into the various theories of play, we must, I think, distinguish between play as a creative activity, and play as withdrawal from a reality which seems too difficult to master. Else Lasker-Schüler's 'Spiellust' is rooted in both aspects, and it must once more be stressed that it is not always possible to sustain the theoretical distinction in studying the phenomenon.

By calling art a 'play', she wished to emphasize how seriously she took it:

> Kunst ist kein Gewerbe, wie auch der Mensch oder ein Tier oder gar ein Gott kein Gewerbe ist. (. . .) Kunst ist keine Beschäftigung, (. . .) Spiel keine Spielerei. Liebelt das Kunstgewerbliche mit der Zierlichkeit des Goldpantöffelchens seiner Stoffpuppen, so ist es mir doch sympathischer, malt der Künstler mal frech und geschmacklos dem Weib des Amenophis einen Schnurrbart an.
> (GW, II, 548–9)

This is a defence of childlike fantasy against childish artiness. Her poetry is particularly rich in such fantasy, the manifestation of creative freedom. Bold metaphors, successful neologism and delightful nonsense verse anticipating dadaist experiments bear witness to the resourcefulness of her 'Spielsprache'.[1] But at this moment we are more concerned with the other side of her 'Spiellust', her attempts 'die Menschheit zu verkindlichen' in which we saw a refusal to accept the claims of a grown-up world.

In *Mein stilles Lied* we have met one example of such a 'Verkindlichung' – 'Denn meine Liebe ist ein Kind und wollte spielen' (see above, p. 45). This longing for a love relationship that has the quality of 'child's play' is expressed also in *Nebel*. The poem starts on a note of hopelessness:

> Wir sitzen traurig Hand in Hand,
> Die gelbe Sonnenrose,
> Die strahlende Braut Gottes,
> Leuchtet erdenabgewandt.

[1] Muschg, *op. cit.* p. 146.

It ends, however, in highspirited playfulness:

> Und was werden wir beide spielen . . .
> Wir halten uns fest umschlungen
> Und kugeln uns über die Erde,
> Über die Erde.   (GW, I, 125)

The intervening stanzas show the process of change from desolation to idyllic contentment: the lovers in their longing become like children ('Und unsere Augen weiten / Sich fragend wie Kinderaugen'), fantasy creates a childhood paradise ('(. . .) du, wir wollen / Wie junge Himmel uns lieben'), despair dissolves into 'rauschende Süße', and love, in the end, becomes play.

In the cycle of poems entitled *Gottfried Benn*, the play imagery is striking. The following poem shows the 'Verkindlichung' in an extreme form:

> *O, Deine Hände*
>
> Sind meine Kinder.
> Alle meine Spielsachen
> Liegen in ihren Gruben.
>
> Immer spiel ich Soldaten
> Mit deinen Fingern, kleine Reiter,
> Bis sie umfallen.
>
> Wie ich sie liebe
> Deine Bubenhände, die zwei.   (GW, I, 203)

One of these poems bears the title *Giselheer dem Knaben* (GW, I, 206), another *Das Lied des Spielprinzen* (GW, I, 209). In *Giselheer dem Tiger*, she calls the beloved one

> Du mein Indianerbuch,
> Wild West,
> Siouxhäuptling!
>
> Im Zwielicht schmachte ich
> Gebunden am Buxbaumstamm –
>
> Ich kann nicht mehr sein
> Ohne das Skalpspiel.   (GW, I, 212)

In the characteristically entitled *Klein Sterbelied*, she turns her
pain over the lover's rejection into a kind of children's prayer:

> Mein Herz noch klein
> Starb leis an Pein.
>
> War blau und fromm!
> O Himmel, komm. (GW, I, 213)

In *Abschied*, a poem from a cycle dedicated to Hans Adalbert
von Maltzahn, marriage can only be seen in a child's setting:

> Aber wenn meine Spieluhren spielen
> Feiern wir Hochzeit. (GW, I, 241)

But this longing for a 'Verkindlichung' of existence goes beyond
the wish for playful love relationships. The ideal relation to the
world, even to God, is sometimes seen as one between playmates:

> Ich und die Erde wurden wie zwei Spielgefährten groß!
> (GW, I, 315)
>
> Kinder waren unsere Seelen,
> Als sie mit dem Leben spielten,
> Wie die Märchen sich erzählen. (GW, I, 141)
>
> Meine erste Blüte Blut sehnte sich nach dir,
> So komme doch,
> Du süßer Gott,
> Du Gespiele Gott,
> Deines Tores Gold schmilzt an meiner Sehnsucht.
> (GW, I, 138)

The first stanza of *Letzter Abend im Jahr* shows, I think, that
Else Lasker-Schüler was not altogether aware of the evasive
aspect of her 'Spiellust':

> Es ist so dunkel heut,
> Man kann kaum in den Abend sehen.
> Ein Lichtchen loht,
> Verspieltes Himmelchen spielt Abendrot
> Und weigert sich, in seine Seligkeit zu gehen.
> – So alt wird jedes Jahr die Zeit –
> Und die vorangegangene verwandelte der Tod.
> (GW, I, 317)

Her own fear of the reality of time seems here projected on to the sky which, by playing 'Abendrot', refuses, so to speak, to grow up. This poem ends, as we have seen, in great seriousness with a question to God:

> O Gott, wie kann der Mensch verstehen,
> Warum der Mensch haltlos vom Menschtum bricht,
> Sich wieder sammeln muß im höheren Geschehen.

At this point, there is no evasion, but a readiness to ask fundamental questions, more moving even for its simplicity. 'Verspieltes Himmelchen' has turned into the 'blausten Himmel in Gottost' (*idem*).

(b) Flight from Identity: ' Masks'

> In der Nacht meiner tiefsten Not erhob ich mich zum Prinzen von
> Theben.   (GW, II, 534–5)

In this laconic statement, contained in one of Else Lasker-Schüler's biographical essays, we meet another aspect of her escape into fantasy. In her 'Briefroman' *Mein Herz* we get some indication of the nature of this 'tiefste Not', that made her withdraw behind the 'mask' of the 'Prince of Thebes': for in this book she describes the break-up of her relationship with Herwarth Walden, and towards the end of it, among the letters addressed to Walden, we find the following 'Telegramm':

> Eben regierender Prinz in Theben geworden. Es lebe die Haupt-
> stadt und mein Volk.   (GW, II, 385)

About this 'mask', Muschg writes:

> Der Prinz von Theben war die neue Maske, die Else Lasker-
> Schüler wählte, nachdem sie in den 'Hebräischen Balladen' das
> Alte Testament als ihre geistige Heimat entdeckt hatte. Die
> Jussufmaske verband das hebräische Kolorit mit dem ägypti-
> schen . . . Jussuf ist der biblische Joseph, der traumkundige
> Liebling Pharaos, der Held jener Geschichte, die Goethe für die
> schönste aller Erzählungen hielt.[1]

[1] Muschg, *op. cit.* p. 126.

The story of Joseph was also her favourite story, and Höltgen mentions a play of hers on this theme completed in 1932 and probably lost during her flight from Germany.[1] In *Das Hebräerland* she tells us how she, the dreamer, was already at school identified with Joseph:

> Ich träume – rügte mich die Lehrerin fast täglich in der Schule – und die Folge davon, ich 'untenan' säße. Meine schwärmerische herrliche Mama behauptete zwar, daß Träumen etwas Seltenes in der Welt. Joseph von Ägypten habe viel geträumt, sogar dem Pharao die Träume gedeutet. Joseph und seine Brüder war meine Lieblingsgeschichte und ich durfte sie immer erzählen in der Religionsstunde. Ich sei ja der Joseph von Ägypten *selbst*, rief eines Tages, ganz dumm, eine Mitschülerin. Darum glaubten es alle Kinder in der Klasse, und mir kam's so vom Himmel hoch herunter; und ich vermochte seitdem gar nicht mehr aufzupassen.
>
> (GW, II, 866)

It would require a study of its own to explore the manifold meaning of the figure of Joseph for Else Lasker-Schüler, and examine the numerous references to him in her prose work. But it is an interesting fact, and one to which we shall return, that her 'masks', among which that of 'Jussuf' was the most important, do not play as big a part in her poetry as one would at first expect, though they dominate her prose. We must therefore be satisfied with the most immediate associations: Joseph the 'outsider' favoured by his father and God, but persecuted by the world, bearer of divine gifts of insight who only after great suffering comes into his own as the provider for those who tried to destroy him. It is not difficult to see why this figure held such great attraction for this poet, and why she identified herself with it. Some writers[2] have stressed the fact of the 'maleness' of this 'mask' without going into the significance of it. It would be interesting, though beyond the scope of this study, to examine the masculine aspects of this poet's personality – here, again, it must suffice to regard the 'maleness' of the chosen 'mask' as a special aspect of her flight from identity.

[1] Höltgen, *op. cit.* p. 28.   [2] Muschg, *op. cit.* p. 126, and Kraft, *op. cit.* p. 9.

There is only one poem in which she refers to herself as 'Joseph' – she does so in a very specific context, and we will consider it at a later point. Meanwhile I suggest a somewhat closer examination of *Heimweh* which, as we shall see, is written in the 'mask' of the '*Prinz von Theben*':

> Ich kann die Sprache
> Dieses kühlen Landes nicht,
> Und seinen Schritt nicht gehn.
>
> Auch die Wolken, die vorbeiziehn,
> Weiß ich nicht zu deuten.
>
> Die Nacht ist eine Stiefkönigin.
>
> Immer muß ich an die Pharaonenwälder denken
> Und küsse die Bilder meiner Sterne.
>
> Meine Lippen leuchten schon
> Und sprechen Fernes,
>
> Und bin ein buntes Bilderbuch
> Auf deinem Schoß.
>
> Aber dein Antlitz spinnt
> Einen Schleier aus Weinen.
>
> Meinen schillernden Vögeln
> Sind die Korallen ausgestochen,
>
> An den Hecken der Gärten
> Versteinern sich ihre weichen Nester.
>
> Wer salbt meine toten Paläste –
> Sie trugen die Kronen meiner Väter,
> Ihre Gebete versanken im heiligen Fluß.   (GW, I, 168)

The first six lines conjure up once more the picture of the exile, but this time it is an exile from a warmer, more mysterious country. Though this country is later given the features of some exotic landscape, it is at the same time the realm of fantasy itself from which the poet feels banned, cast out into an everyday reality, the language of which she does not understand. As before, night appears as a hostile force: the neologism 'Stiefkönigin' alludes both to the speaker's noble birth, anticipating the last line but one, and to another aspect of his banishment,

the separation from his true mother. (I say 'his' on the assumption that the poet speaks here in the 'mask' of 'Jussuf'.)

The first line of the next stanza establishes Egypt as the
country of the speaker's origin. 'Und küsse die Bilder meiner
Sterne' is not easy to interpret. We have met the star as a symbol
of transcending grace, and perhaps we are meant to imagine the
'Prince' nostalgically 'kissing' those signs of a power temporarily
hidden – almost as any refugee may caress some souvenirs which
he has brought with him from the country he had to leave. Else
Lasker-Schüler made a number of drawings of herself as 'Jussuf'
(see DD, illustration opposite title-page), and these show her
face decorated by moon and star: for these drawings Muschg's
interpretation that 'der "Stern im Angesicht" ist schlechthin das
Zeichen der Auserwählten'[1] seems very apt, and would lend
support to my understanding of this difficult line.

The next two lines can perhaps be taken as a consequence of
the preceding one: the lips, having come into contact with the
healing power that is now remote, begin to 'glow' and speak
of the realm that is lost. The subsequent lines bring a sudden
turn to a personal situation: the speaker addresses someone,
presumably some beloved person. At this point, a play element
enters ('ein buntes Bilderbuch') and adds 'Verkindlichung' to
flight from identity as another means of escape into fantasy. But
the person to whom the child-prince speaks remains inaccessible,
separated from him by a veil of tears; the reason for these tears
is not disclosed.

The next four lines form a unit: the desolation and lostness
of the exile is expressed through the potent image of the birds
whose eyes have been put out (I think the 'und ausgestochen'
permits us to interpret 'Korallen' here as coral eyes), and whose
nests have turned to stone. The image is extraordinarily rich in
meaning: birds have been, throughout the history of mankind,
symbols of the spirit, divine messengers who connect the higher
and lower regions of being, and their nests carry associations of
warmth and security; blind birds in stone nests convey most

[1] Muschg, *op. cit.* p. 139.

powerfully a sense of complete disorientation. That Else Lasker-Schüler's birds are obviously of an exotic nature ('schillernd', 'Korallen') makes them inhabitants of that far-off mysterious country for which the exiled speaker yearns.

The last stanza finally establishes the speaker's 'identity' – he is the owner of palaces, and he and his 'Väter' were wearing crowns. It is this, together with the memories of 'Pharaonen-wälder', that reveals her 'mask' in this poem as that of 'Jussuf, Prince of Thebes'. Once again, a picture of spiritual death emerges: the signs of the prince's nobility are no longer 'anointed', grace has departed from them, the prayers are dead.

She adopted a less solemn version of the 'mask' of the 'Spielprinz' in some of her poems to Benn, as we have already seen (see above, p. 70). The poem *Giselheer dem Knaben*, in a much more concentrated form, sounds some of the themes of *Heimweh*:

> An meiner Wimper hängt ein Stern,
> Es ist so hell
> Wie soll ich schlafen –
>
> Und möchte mit dir spielen.
> – Ich habe keine Heimat –
> Wir spielen König und Prinz.   (GW, I, 206)

Here too, I feel, the star 'an meinen Wimpern' is a disturbing reminder of what is lost ('Ich habe keine Heimat'). The difference is, however, that we come here across the very process of 'mask-making': the poet suggests the play of 'König und Prinz' as an escape from homelessness, thus bearing out the truth of Muschg's suggestion: 'Von Anfang an war dieses Märchengeflunker ein Heilmittel gegen die Schwermut gewesen.'[1]

In a few poems, Else Lasker-Schüler speaks also as a 'Prinzessin'. The creation of the 'mask' of the Princess 'Tino von Baghdad' preceded that of 'Jussuf' – it seems that the name 'Tino' was invented for her by Peter Hille (GW, II, 9). But though 'Jussuf' became her favourite 'mask', she continued to sign some of her letters with 'Tino'. In a poem which she wrote for the 'King of

---

[1] *Ibid.* p. 129.

Bohemia' – which was a 'mask' she created for the writer Paul Leppin – she says:

> Aus dem Gold meiner Stirne leuchtet der Smaragd,
> Der den Sommer färbt.
> Ich bin eine Prinzessin.   (GW, I, 230)

And another poem addressed to Paul Leppin shows that some of the poet's friends were ready to 'play' with her:

> Der König von Böhmen
> Schenkte mir seine Dichtung Daniel Jesus.
> Ich schlug sie auf und las: Der lieben, lieben, lieben, lieben Prinzessin.
>   (GW, I, 229)

'Dressing up' was for Else Lasker-Schüler by no means just a literary attitude. Benn, in his talk about the poet in 1952, gives a vivid description of her appearance at the time of their friendship:

> Man konnte weder damals noch später mit ihr über die Straße gehen, ohne daß alle Welt stillstand und ihr nachsah: extravagante weite Röcke oder Hosen, unmögliche Obergewänder, Hals und Arme behängt mit auffallendem unechtem Schmuck, Ketten, Ohrringen, Talmiringen an den Fingern, und da sie sich unaufhörlich die Haarsträhnen aus der Stirn strich, waren diese, man muß schon sagen: Dienstmädchenringe immer in aller Blickpunkt. Sie aß nie regelmäßig, sie aß sehr wenig, und sie war immer arm in allen Lebenslagen und zu allen Zeiten. Das war der Prinz von Theben, Jussuf, Tino von Bagdad, der schwarze Schwan.[1]

There is a poem *An zwei Freunde* in which she sketches her own image:

> Es schwimmen Tränen braun um meinen Mandelkern
> Und meine Schellen spielen süß am Kleiderrand.
>
> Ich trage einen wilden Kork im Ohrlapp,
> Und Monde tätowiert auf meiner Hand.
> Versteinte Käfer fallen von der Schnur ab.   (GW, I, 232)

The fact that, by thus 'dressing up', she actually tried to live the exotic image she had designed for herself, shows that the

---

[1] Benn, *op. cit.* pp. 537–8.

'masks' which her writings present were more than just metaphors. The flight from her own identity was not only a poetic
device. Martini's statement that

> Alle ihre Verse sind nichts als Spiegelungen, Bekenntnisse,
> Verzauberungen dieser poetischen Existenz, die sie über ihrem
> armen gehetzten und entbehrungsreichen Erdendasein phantasie-
> voll ausspann[1]

is an over-simplification. It seems to propose a complete dicho-
tomy between a life too difficult to bear, and a poetry which
serves as an escape from it. We have, however, seen that her life
itself contained many elements of fantastication while the conflict
between a flight from and a confrontation with reality seems to
me the very essence of her poetry, and is the theme of this study.
If the 'mask', though a predominant element in her prose, plays
a comparatively minor part in her verse, it is, perhaps, because
she came nearer to 'being herself' in poetry than anywhere else.
This brings us to the *Hebräische Balladen*. Kraft writes:

> Sie stellte sich selbst dar ... und wurde doch trotz dieser ineinander
> sich verschiebenden Masken und Mäntel, weil sie ihr Ich ver-
> bergen mußte, um es voll aussprechen zu können, zur Dichterin
> der 'Hebräischen Balladen'.[2]

But he does not seem to use the term 'Masken' here in the same
sense as we do. The *Hebräische Balladen*, as we have seen earlier
(see above, p. 58), are mostly re-creations of biblical tales, by
means of which the poet distances and objectifies her own concerns, longings and fears. The 'I' is here not 'hidden' in the sense
that it hides behind a 'mask' in order not to be seen: it has, so
to speak, stepped behind its creation. This is, to some extent,
the essence of the artistic process: it is not a flight from reality
but objectification of one's involvement in it.

The Joseph of *Joseph wird verkauft* (GW, I, 298) is not the
same figure as 'Jussuf': he is the biblical Joseph, and not the
exotic 'Spielkaiser' whom Else Lasker-Schüler presents as her

[1] F. Martini, *Was war Expressionismus?*, Urach, 1948, p. 108.
[2] Kraft, *op. cit.* p. 9.

alter ego in *Der Prinz von Theben* and *Der Malik*. He is still the outcast ('da er für des Vaters Liebe büßte') who prevails in the end through his power of imagination ('An seinem Traume hingen aller Deutung Garben') but he is left his own story, his own fate: the poet's 'I' does not intrude. The same is true of Abel, Jacob, Saul and other figures in this cycle.

There are, however, a few poems where this is not so clear. In them the biblical figures themselves speak, and the question arises: is this only a dramatic version of the same attempt at 'distancing', or is the poet here speaking through a chosen 'mask'? Let us look at the beginning of *Pharao und Joseph*:

> Pharao verstößt seine blühenden Weiber,
> Sie duften nach den Gärten Amons.
>
> Sein Königskopf ruht auf meiner Schulter,
> Die strömt Korngeruch aus.   (GW, I, 299)

Joseph is speaking, and his relation with Pharaoh is interpreted as a love relationship. But daring though this may seem, it does not necessarily turn the biblical Joseph into the 'mask' of 'Jussuf'. But if we look at the end of the poem –

> Aber sein träumerisch Herz
> Rauscht auf meinem Grund.
>
> Darum dichten meine Lippen
> Große Süßigkeiten,
> Im Weizen unseres Morgens   (*ibid.*)

we are reminded of some of Else Lasker-Schüler's most intimate love poems, particularly the one poem in which she calls herself Joseph and which is addressed to Benn, *Dem Barbaren*. I quote the last three stanzas:

> Ich bin Joseph und trage einen süßen Gürtel
> Um meine bunte Haut.
>
> Dich beglückt das erschrockene Rauschen
> Meiner Muscheln.
>
> Aber dein Herz läßt keine Meere mehr ein.
> O du!   (GW, I, 221)

79

The three other poems in *Hebräische Balladen* which are, as it were, dramatic monologues – the two in which David speaks about his friendship with Jonathan, and the one called *Ruth* – raise a similar question: all three are, like *Pharao und Joseph*, very close in tone and feeling to her love poetry. *Ruth* in particular could easily find a place among the poet's love poems – only the last line reveals the identity of the speaker for which nothing that went before had prepared us:

> Und du suchst mich vor den Hecken.
> Ich höre deine Schritte seufzen
> Und meine Augen sind schwere dunkle Tropfen.
>
> In meiner Seele blühen süß deine Blicke
> Und füllen sich,
> Wenn meine Augen in den Schlaf wandeln.
>
> Am Brunnen meiner Heimat
> Steht ein Engel,
> Der singt das Lied meiner Liebe,
> Der singt das Lied Ruths. (GW, I, 308)

I do not feel I can give a conclusive answer to the question whether in these poems Else Lasker-Schüler speaks to us through a 'mask', or whether she has created in them symbols that concretely, and independent of herself, give universal expression to her individual experience. But I am inclined to think that the very attempt to find 'objective correlatives' for her experience expresses the wish to meet rather than to escape from herself.

(4) *Preoccupation with Death*

We conclude our examination of the various manifestations of Else Lasker-Schüler's tendency to withdraw from reality with a consideration of her preoccupation with the idea of death. Seventy-two of the 316 poems and fragments so far published contain at least one reference to death, and in the first poem she ever published, *Verwelkte Myrten*, which appeared in 1899 in the periodical *Die Gesellschaft*, we already find the characteristic lines:

> – Mir war, wie ich an deiner Seite lag,
> Als ob mein Herze sich nicht mehr bewegt. (GW, III, 133)

80

These references are, however, of varying kind. Beside what we may perhaps call 'death wishes', there are descriptions of mental states characterized by a feeling of a 'death-in-life'. These too show fairly unambiguously the more or less conscious desire to withdraw from a reality that is experienced as alien and hostile: their nature is 'regressive' in the sense in which we used this Freudian term earlier on (see above, p. 44). But there are other poems in which a more ambivalent idea of death emerges: as we have previously seen (see above, pp. 55 and 63–4), it is at the point of extreme withdrawal that the direction of the pendulum may change – the 'dark night of the soul' may become the transition to a new understanding and acceptance, and death itself may be seen as the carrier of a seed of new birth.

There are, finally, poems where the conquest of death is celebrated. Though, theoretically speaking, these do not belong in this section, I should nevertheless like to include them as a reminder that no scheme can be adequate to the reality of things: in poetry, as in life, withdrawal and outgoing impulses go together.

Death Wishes

Kühle

In den weißen Gluten
Der hellen Rosen
Möchte ich verbluten.

Doch auf den Teichen
Warten die starren, seelenlosen Wasserrosen,
Um meiner Sehnsucht Kühle zu reichen.   (GW, I, 38)

This short poem, in its extreme concentration, is difficult to paraphrase. The poet seems confronted by two kinds of self-destruction – bleeding to death, and drowning. What these two have in common is indicated by the title – *Kühle*, a cooling down of the poet's painful longing. In the first three lines, this longing runs out, so to speak, with her life-blood and is absorbed by the 'weiße Gluten' of roses. But, as if these flowers were still too alive, not 'cool' enough (for though their glow is 'white', they still glow!), the poet turns to the 'starren, seelenlosen Wasserrosen' which – in their lifeless rigidity, true flowers of death – are more likely to lay her desire to rest. Death by drowning seems to promise the longed-for relief.

The poem clearly shows the impulse behind her 'death wishes' – a longing for the end of longing and, in a wider sense, for the end of that constant tension which is the very essence of living. We are reminded of the passages in which Freud, in *Jenseits des Lustprinzips*, announces his discovery of the 'Todestrieb', e.g.

> Daß wir als die herrschende Tendenz des Seelenlebens, vielleicht des Nervenlebens überhaupt, das Streben nach Herabsetzung, Konstanterhaltung, Aufhebung der inneren Reizspannung erkannten (das Nirwanaprinzip nach einem Ausdruck von Barbara Low), wie es im Lustprinzip zum Ausdruck kommt, das ist ja eines unserer stärksten Motive, an die Existenz von Todestrieben zu glauben.[1]

This theory of a 'death instinct', in opposition to and balance with a 'life instinct', has been passionately contested even by some of Freud's followers. I do not wish to enter the controversy which is still raging about the merit of this hypothesis. But the proposition of a self-destructive urge, presenting an extreme manifestation of the wish to withdraw from a reality so painful to bear, seems to me entirely justified – for whatever its metaphysical implications, here is a psychological phenomenon we can all observe.

In *Kühle* the longing for death is more indicated than pronounced – even the expression 'verbluten' can still be taken metaphorically. In other poems, suicidal fantasies are expressed more directly. We have already met the 'death wish' in connection with Else Lasker-Schüler's emotional involvement with her mother in the early *Resignation* which ends:

> Und sehne mich nach ew'ger Nacht.
> Zu schmelzen still im Abendrot,
> In deinem Heilandarme, Tod.   (See above, p. 68)

[1] S. Freud, *Gesammelte Schriften*, Bd. VI, Wien, 1925, p. 248.

Here the influence of German romanticism, with its 'Todeskult', is very obvious. *Verinnerlicht*, a much later poem, opens on a more direct, more personal note:

> Ich denke immer ans Sterben.
> Mich hat niemand lieb. (GW, I, 217)

This poem points at the very roots of the poet's despair which here leads to the 'death wish': love is the 'home' from which she feels eternally exiled:

> Weiß nicht wo ich hin soll
> Wie überall zu dir.
> Bist meine heimliche Heimat (. . .) (*ibid.*)

These simple lines express the core of this poet's tragic 'split' – between the deep awareness of the healing and transcending power of erotic contact and her failure to achieve it.

Outside her poetry, her frequent references to suicide often have a self-mocking, ironical quality, a taste of 'Galgenhumor', which makes them appear more destructive, more removed from the sources of the despair which feeds them:

> Cardinal! Ich habe mich nun zum wiederholten MAL erhängt –
> wer schnitt mich immer ab – kleine grobe Fäden hängen nun an mir
> mit dem Preis. Ich lach, ich bin nix mehr wert. (BK, p. 88)

> Es war an einem Abend, abgemagert kam der Mond, zu leben
> hat es sich für ihn und auch für mich nicht mehr gelohnt und
> wir beschlossen, da die Spree gut temperiert, uns beide zu ersäufen.
> Auf – und ausprobiert! Mein Selbstmord wäre außerdem meinen
> Verlegern zur stattlichen Reklame willkommen gewesen und
> ich fühle mich seit der Unterlassung irgendwie ihnen verpflichtet!
> (GW, II, 538–9)

As in her use of 'masks', it is in her poetry that she came closest to an awareness, and thus to an acceptance, of the true nature of her conflict. This becomes very striking if we compare the cynical tone of these prose quotations with that of a poem such as

> *O ich möcht aus der Welt*
> Dann weinst du um mich.
> Blutbuchen schüren
> Meine Träume kriegerisch.
>
> Durch finster Gestrüpp
> Muß ich
> Und Gräben und Wasser.
>
> Immer schlägt wilde Welle
> An mein Herz;
> Innerer Feind.
>
> O ich möchte aus der Welt!
> Aber auch fern von ihr
> Irr ich, ein Flackerlicht
>
> Um Gottes Grab.   (GW, I, 222)

The title, as in others of her poems, is at the same time part of the first stanza and theme of the whole poem. Together with the second line it expresses a familiar and still rather narrow thought: once she is dead, the lover will cry for her. The remaining lines of this stanza form a thematic unit with the next two stanzas: in vivid images which defy prose transcription the poet conjures up the dream landscape into which she withdraws, and which is as violent ('Blutbuchen schüren / Meine Träume kriegerisch') and as hostile ('Innerer Feind') as the 'world' on which she wishes to turn her back. We have here an astonishing poetic representation of the psychological process of depression: rejection of the outside world is turned inwards and experienced, even physically, as an inner violence ('Immer schlägt wilde Welle / An mein Herz').

In the remaining four lines, the first of which repeats the theme, we reach an altogether deeper level, and the true ground of the poet's despair is revealed: it is no longer the lover's rejection, but the death of God – and from that there is no escape. The last isolated line 'Um Gottes Grab' is like a sudden, painful but liberating illumination of the dark confusion that precedes it.

Death-in-Life

In our section on 'Despair and Isolation' we have already encountered Else Lasker-Schüler's attempts to give expression to the experience of a mental state we have called 'death-in-life'. We found this at the beginning of the poem in which the poet sees herself as an aimless wanderer:

> Ich liege wo am Wegrand übermattet –
> Und über mir die finstere kalte Nacht –
> Und zähl schon zu den Toten längst bestattet.
>
> (See above, p. 48)

We also met it in that stanza in *Chaos* which we saw as an expression of existential anxiety:

> Ich finde mich nicht wieder
> In dieser Todverlassenheit!
> Mir ist: ich lieg' von mir weltenweit
> Zwischen grauer Nacht der Urangst . . .
>
> (See above, p. 52)

This feeling of being 'längst bestattet', 'lange schon gestorben' (GW, I, 225), recurs like a leitmotif throughout her writings. Thus she exclaims on a postcard to Kraus:

> Ich bin immer so traurig und so besorgt, ich bin wie tot. Ich weiß nur eins daß Leben und Tod Hand in Hand gehen, Leben stirbt und Tod ist vergeßlich zum Leben.   (BK, p. 65)

A year later, in a letter, she writes:

> (. . .) aber ich kann nicht mehr kämpfen, ich bin gestorben im Wirrwarr der Welt (. . .)   (*ibid.* p. 79)

We remember how, in *Weltflucht*, 'Wirrwarr', confusion, expressed an inevitable aspect of reality from which the poet often longed to escape.

In her autobiographical essay *Ich räume auf*, the following passage shows once more her preoccupation with death in connection with the image of her mother:

> Dann kam der Mai, den ich so gerne habe, aber Ihnen meine Trostlosigkeit zu schildern (. . .) fehlt mir jede Rücksichtslosigkeit. Ich lag wo in einer Ecke der Straße zwischen Halensee und

Grunewald unbegraben, heimatlos noch im Tode. Ein einfacher
Spatz setzte sich auf meinen Fuß, er gab sich alle Mühe, mir etwas
vorzusingen, ein Garten blühte schon und meiner Mutter Wolke
besprengte meine fiebernde Stirn (. . .)   (GW, II, 541)

The poem *Winternacht*, with the subtitle 'Cellolied', embodies
this experience of 'death-in-life' in comparatively pure form:

> Ich schlafe tief in starrer Winternacht,
> Mir ist, ich lieg' in Grabesnacht,
> Als ob ich spät um Mitternacht gestorben sei
> Und schon ein Sternenleben tot sei.
>
> Zu meinem Kinde zog mein Glück
> Und alles Leiden in das Leid zurück,
> Nur meine Sehnsucht sucht sich heim
> Und zuckt wie zähes Leben
> Und stirbt zurück
>   In sich.
>
> Ich schlafe tief in starrer Winternacht,
> Mir ist, ich lieg' in Grabesnacht.   (GW, I, 22)

The first stanza, the first two lines of which also recur as a kind of
refrain at the end of the poem, is fairly straightforward. We are
familiar with 'Nacht' as a symbol of estrangement; here in the
triple variation 'Winternacht – Grabesnacht – Mitternacht' it is
directly associated with the idea of death. Else Lasker-Schüler's
inclination to absolutize and mythify her emotional experience
is shown by the phrase 'schon ein Sternenleben tot'.

The middle stanza is more complex. The state of spiritual
death is devoid of all feeling, suffering as well as joy. The poet
describes the departure of her feelings in a rather elliptical
manner: her happiness resides now in her child (this is an earlier
poem, and her son was still alive) but she does not seem to have
any share in it; her sufferings have returned into 'das Leid',
some kind of primary suffering – a difficult thought. All that is
left is her longing, most tenacious of her emotional antennae,
but now also dying, twitching, so to speak, in a vacuum, thrown
back upon herself. (The second, later version of this poem ending
at this point with 'und stirbt', omitting 'in sich zurück', weakens

the powerful metaphor. GW, I, 88.) The ambiguity of the word 'heimsuchen' – meaning 'afflict, punish' but also literally 'looking for home' – points at the core of the 'disease' from which the poet 'dies'; where longing finds no other 'home' but itself, its 'death' is certain.

The experience of 'death-in-life' finds a more specific expression in a number of love poems where it appears in the form of variations on the 'Liebestod'-motif. Thus, for instance, in a poem to Hans Ehrenbaum-Degele whom she addressed as 'Tristan':

Als ich Tristan kennenlernte

O,
Du mein Engel,
Wir schweben nur noch
In holden Wolken.

Ich weiß nicht, ob ich lebe
Oder süß gestorben bin
In deinem Herzen.

Immer feiern wir Himmelfahrt
Und viel, viel Schimmer.

Goldene Heiligenbilder
Sind deine Augen.

Sage – wie ich bin?
Überall wollen Blumen aus mir.   (GW, I, 194)

This poem does not need close analysis. The state of love cele-brated here is totally removed from all earthly concerns – it is a 'death' very different from that of *Winternacht*, a 'sweet' death, the death of ecstasy. What these two forms of 'death-in-life' have in common is the aura of unreality.

The next poem in this cycle dedicated to 'Meinem reinen Liebesfreund Hans Ehrenbaum-Degele', this time called *An den Gralprinzen* but in all probability meant for the same man (did she perhaps confuse Tristan with Parzival?), ends characteristi-cally with the lines:

Von Sternen sind wir eingerahmt
Und flüchten aus der Welt.
Ich glaube wir sind Engel.   (GW, I, 195)

In *Das Wunderlied*, these two aspects of 'death-in-life', the cold numbness of *Winternacht* and the sweet ecstasy of the Tristan-poems, are contrasted. Feeling rejected by her lover, the poet complains:

> Süß mir, wenn ich im Rauschen der Liebe
> Für dich gestorben wär –
>
> Nun ist mein Leben verschneit,
> Erstarrt meine Seele (. . .) (GW, I, 320)

The choice seems to be between two different kinds of unreality: the flight into the fantasy of 'Liebestod', and the withdrawal into despair and spiritual death.

The actual death of those who were close to the poet affected her deeply. Astrid Gehlhoff-Claes writes:

> Der Verlust geliebter Menschen durch den Tod löst immer die ohnehin intensive Vorstellung des eignen Todes neu aus, wenn Vereinsamung und Lebensfremdheit die Zurückgebliebene noch mehr als sonst befallen. (BK, p. 163)

This is true, but when considering the poems she wrote on the death of her friends we must, I think, again distinguish between poems where the death of a friend brought out her own 'death wishes', and others where she expressed her grief most movingly without identifying herself with the dead. Such an example of what we have earlier called 'objectification' is her poem on Georg Trakl from which I quote the conclusion:

> Seine dreifaltige Seele trug er in der Hand,
> Als er in den heiligen Krieg zog.
>
> – Dann wußte ich, er war gestorben –
>
> Sein Schatten weilte unbegreiflich
> Auf dem Abend meines Zimmers. (GW, I, 256)

This contrasts strikingly with the following poem on the death of her friend Senna Hoy (whose real name was Johannes Holzman and who died in a Russian prison under the suspicion of revolutionary activities):

Sascha

Um deine Lippen blüht noch jung
Der Trotz dunkelrot,

Aber auf deiner Stirne sind meine Gebete
Vom Sturm verwittert.

Daß wir uns im Leben
Nie küssen sollten . . .

Nun bist du der Engel,
Der auf meinem Grab steht.

Das Atmen der Erde bewegt
Meinen Leib wie lebendig.

Mein Herz scheint hell
Vom Rosenblut der Hecken.

Aber ich bin tot, Sascha,
Und das Lächeln liegt abgepflückt
Nur noch kurz auf meinem Gesicht. (GW, I, 188)

In this poem, a strange reversal has taken place: it is the poet
who is dead and it is only the life around her ('Das Atmen der
Erde', 'Rosenblut der Hecken') which makes her appear alive
while the lover who has in fact died seems full of life ('Um deine
Lippen blüht noch jung / Der Trotz dunkelrot').

The next poem in the cycle dedicated to 'Meinem so geliebten
Spielgefährten Senna Hoy' (we note again the element of
'Verkindlichung'!) takes up the same theme:

Jede Schaufel Erde, die dich barg,
Verschüttete auch mich. (GW, I, 189)

But the beginning of the poem introduces another note:

Seit du begraben liegst auf dem Hügel,
Ist die Erde süß.

Wo ich hingehe nun auf Zehen,
Wandele ich über reine Wege.

O deines Blutes Rosen
Durchtränken sanft den Tod.

Ich habe keine Furcht mehr
vor dem Sterben. (*ibid.*)

89

Not only has the idea of death become easier to bear now that the friend has died, but life itself has become transfigured: the earth has become 'sweet', the roads 'pure'. Death has been taken into life, 'death-in-life' has become a cosmic experience.

Death as Transition

Dasein

Hatte wogendes Nachthaar,
Liegt lange schon wo begraben.
Hatte zwei Augen wie Bäche klar,
Bevor die Trübsal mein Gast war,
Hatte Hände muschelrotweiß,
Aber die Arbeit verzehrte ihr Weiß.
Und einmal kommt der Letzte,
Der senkt den unabänderlichen Blick
Nach meines Leibes Vergänglichkeit
Und wirft von mir alles Sterben.
Und es atmet meine Seele auf
Und trinkt das Ewige . . .   (GW, I, 30)

The first six lines of this poem sound a theme familiar from the previous section – the 'death-in-life' motif appears this time in the balladesque form which Else Lasker-Schüler frequently chose in earlier work – another link with the Romantic movement! But the seventh line introduces a new idea. The state of being buried alive is changed by someone whom the poet calls 'der Letzte' and who divests the 'speaker' of 'alles Sterben'. The state that is now reached is, however, not a return to the old life. The last two lines hint at a new state of being, a mystical awareness of eternity, a point beyond life and death. Here the experience of spiritual death brought about by 'Trübsal' is only a transition to a heightened awareness, a kind of new birth. What this 'Trübsal' is, is not clearly said – perhaps poverty ('Aber die Arbeit verzehrte ihr Weiß'), perhaps betrayal through a lover. The identity of 'der Letzte' is also left open – perhaps we are meant to associate the 'last lover' which, in the context of the poem, could only be God. This points to the second part of our study where we shall see to what extent the search for God is, in fact, the 'outgoing' aspect of her.

Turning once more from death as a fantasy to the experience of actual death, we can discover this other forward-pointing note too. We already found two different kinds of poems on the death of others – those which like the poems on Senna Hoy show the poet drawn into her 'death wishes', and others like the poems on Trakl which express her grief without any identification with the dead (see above, pp. 88–9). In *An mein Kind* we meet yet another reaction to actual death, the death of the person whom she loved most deeply, her son Paul. This death affected her as no other, and the pain it caused did not diminish over the years:

> Immer wieder wirst du mir
> Im scheidenden Jahre sterben, mein Kind,
>
> Wenn das Laub zerfließt
> Und die Zweige schmal werden. (. . .)
>
> Darum weine ich sehr, ewiglich . . .
> In der Nacht meines Herzens.
>
> Noch seufzen aus mir die Schlummerlieder,
> Die dich in den Todesschlaf schluchzten,
>
> Und meine Augen wenden sich nicht mehr
> Der Welt zu;
>
> Das Grün des Laubes tut ihnen weh.   (GW, I, 335)

Up to this point the poem is simple and a very real expression of a mother's mourning for her child, though it gains a special dimension through the fact that it appeared sixteen years after Paul's death. The following line, however, brings a change of feeling:

> – Aber der Ewige wohnt in mir.   (*ibid.*)

The experience of death has led to an awareness of God, the backward swing of the pendulum is arrested, a new view opened up. This is made more concrete in the following two lines:

> Die Liebe zu dir ist das Bildnis,
> Das man sich von Gott machen darf.   (*ibid.*)

Her love for her child could easily have led to a rejection of God – what could be more difficult to accept than the death of a highly gifted son at the age of twenty-seven? But in this poem it is, on the contrary, the very depth of this love which helps her to discern the 'image' of God – an 'image' which she feels permitted to 'make' because it is not a material image, not an idol. In this 'correction' of the Old Testament commandment, the Jewish poet reveals her concern with distinctly Christian values.

The remainder of the poem returns to the mood of mourning, a note of gentle sadness, far removed from the self-destructive fantasies of, e.g., Senna Hoy (see above, p. 89). Though the breaking-in of the 'image' of God into the dark world of grief is not explored any further, it suffuses the whole poem with a strange light which gives it a kind of transparency.

The experience of death as a way to an awareness of eternal values – this conception emerges also from some poems in which Else Lasker-Schüler anticipates her own death. Thus, she writes in *Herbst*:

> Ich pflücke mir am Weg das letzte Tausendschön . . .
> Es kam ein Engel mir mein Totenkleid zu nähen –
> Denn ich muß andere Welten weiter tragen.
>
> Das ewige Leben *dem*, der viel von Liebe weiß zu sagen.
> Ein Mensch der *Liebe* kann nur auferstehen!
> Haß schachtelt ein! wie hoch die Fackel auch mag schlagen.
>
> (GW, I, 351)

Here the idea of resurrection enters, and though it is at first presented in a strange garb reminiscent of the reincarnation concepts of Oriental mysticism ('Denn ich muß andere Welten weiter tragen'), the two lines that follow present a view that is very close to Christianity. Just as it is the depth of her love for Paul, that in spite of his death, brings her to a realization of the 'image' of God, it is through the power of love that death, instead of being a final state of desolation, becomes a transition to another kind of being.

In poems like these her preoccupation with death presents

itself neither as self-destructive rejection of, nor as romantic escape from, a painful reality but as a transitional stage on the way to a new awareness, a new 'birth' – whether 'death' is the symbolic expression of spiritual desolation, or as in *Herbst* is anticipated in its full actuality.

Conquest of Death

We find, however, yet another approach to death in Else Lasker-Schüler's poetry where death is experienced as a threat whose very existence has to be challenged:

Jugend

Ich hört Dich hämmern diese Nacht
An einem Sarg im tiefen Erdenschacht.
Was willst Du von mir, Tod!
Mein Herz spielt mit dem jungen Morgenrot
Und tanzt im Funkenschwarm der Sonnenglut
Mit all den Blumen und der Sommerlust.

Scheer' Dich des Weges, alter Nimmersatt!
Was soll ich in der Totenstadt,
Ich, mit dem Jubel in der Brust.   (GW, I, 55)

An examination of Else Lasker-Schüler's preoccupation with death would be incomplete without this aspect of defiance of the destructive, disintegrating forces. This is the point where opposites live side by side, and where the whole complexity of the poet's involvement with the 'world' can be perhaps most clearly seen. The same person who so frequently played with the idea of suicide could say when hearing about Stefan Zweig's death:

Nur einen Augenblick . . . einen Augenblick nur noch . . . im nächsten hätte er es ja nicht mehr getan.   (DD, p. 597)

The same person whose many-shaped death fantasies we have tried to trace could end a poem with the words: 'Ich will nicht sterben!' (GW, I, 59).

The means by which death can be conquered is love – just as it is the failure of love that, we have seen, leads to death. In a story, she describes how she brought back to life a beloved

93

butterfly that seemed dead – she did so by 'playing God', that is, by breathing on it until it moved its wings again and flew up into the sky (GW, ɪɪ, 666ff.). The theme of the story is the one-ness of breath (=life), love and God. There are a number of poems which express this old, and again very Christian, idea of love as the conqueror of death. Here are quotations from some of them:

> Ich wollte, Du und ich, wir würden uns verzweigen,
> Wenn sonnentoll der Sommertag nach Regen schreit
> Und Wetterwolken bersten in der Luft!
> Und alles Leben wäre unser Eigen;
> Den Tod selbst rissen wir aus seiner Gruft
> Und jubelten durch seine Schweigsamkeit!   (GW, ɪ, 33)

> Und Immergrün schlingen wir um den Tod
> Und geben ihm Leben.   (GW, ɪ, 52)

> Wir wollen uns versöhnen die Nacht,
> Wenn wir uns herzen, sterben wir nicht.   (GW, ɪ, 155)

> Alles ist tot,
> Nur du und ich nicht.   (GW, ɪ, 204)

Love as the conqueror of death. At this point we cross over from withdrawal to outgoing, having reached the reversal of the movement which this first part of our examination tried to outline – a movement which led from failure of love to disappointment and resentment, to despair and isolation, and from there on to the various forms of escape from a loveless world, the flight into childhood and behind 'masks', and finally the withdrawal from the painful confusion of life into fantasies about the painless 'peace' of death.

Thus we found the pendulum swinging further and further backwards, away from any contact with reality, but unlike a real pendulum reaching in the end a point where the experience of greatest distance, of 'death' in its various manifestations, can also become the point of a new departure – this time into the 'opposite' direction, forwards, in search of contact, reality, meaning. It is this movement which the second part of our study will attempt to follow.

(B) THE FORWARD MOVEMENT: OUTGOING

(1) *Longing for Contact*

In our exploration of Else Lasker-Schüler's withdrawal from reality in its varying manifestation and intensity, we discovered again and again a deep longing for contact, and saw in her despair over her inability to achieve it the very impulse behind her frequent rejection of life, her 'backward' movement. I stressed at the beginning that the decision to consider her escape from contact *before* her attempts to reach contact was, to some extent, arbitrary – that both withdrawal from and search for contact were aspects of the same deep and overwhelming need. It was Else Lasker-Schüler's demand for a complete union, for an 'all-or-nothing', to which others would not and could not respond, that made her frequently recoil from a world which – since it was not wholly friendly – was experienced as wholly hostile.

If I have nevertheless chosen to present my examination in this order – letting the forward movement of the pendulum *follow* the backward one – it is, as I said, because the highest manifestation of her search for contact, the search for God, brought her closest to a reconciliation of the opposing forces: here the demand for 'all-or-nothing' was finally abandoned, and the limitations of the human condition accepted.

In an essay, *Freundschaft und Liebe*, which offers many important clues for our theme, the poet puts the loss of her mother at the root of her longing:

> Wenn man keine Mutter mehr hat, in deren Liebe sich Himmel und
> Erde verklären, wünscht man sich sehnlichst einen guten Freund,
> eine gute Freundin. (GW, II, 611)

Here is an ideal image which, like all such images, carries the seed of disappointment, a disappointment which is anticipated in the next sentence:

> Man weiß allerdings, 'ist man sich Freund', wen man hat! An
> Eigentreue erlebt man selten eine Enttäuschung. (*ibid.*)

In these two sentences, we find in a nutshell the whole 'history, of her longing for human contact: as the perfection of the relationship between mother and child can never be repeated, disappointment is inevitable, and the only protection against it is 'Eigentreue' which, though meaning literally 'faithfulness towards oneself', carries here also the additional meaning of 'self-relatedness'.

A few sentences later, however, the necessity of an 'encounter' with another person, a friend or a lover, is stressed once more:

> Doch die Erfüllung aller Sehnsucht nach Freundschaft bedeutet,
> die Begegnung seines zweiten Gesichts. Den Freund verlangt
> es immer, im Freund sein Ebenbild zu sehen, wie der Liebende
> in der Herzallerliebsten seine Vollendung.   (*ibid.*)

The longing for the 'Begegnung seines zweiten Gesichts', and the fear of disappointment leading to a 'Vorliebnehmen' (*ibid.*) with oneself, are the two poles between which Else Lasker-Schüler's emotional life swings. But the wish to find one's 'home' in another is never absent for long, a wish which is expressed in *Rast*:

> Mit einem stillen Menschen will ich wandern
> Über die Berge meiner Heimat,
> Schluchzend über Schluchten,
> Über hingestreckte Lüfte.
>
> Überall beugen sich die Zedern
> Und streuen Blüten.
>
> Aber meine Schulter hängt herab
> Von der Last des Flügels.
> Suche ewige, stille Hände:
> Mit meiner Heimat will ich wandern.   (GW, I, 170)

The title expresses the wish for a release from the tension of living which, as the first line indicates, can come about through the companionship of another person: this person can be 'still', it is his or her presence that matters, not what is spoken. The third line implies that such companionship does not necessarily eliminate the pain and difficulty of the journey but – if I understand the symbolism of the bowing tree in the second stanza rightly – it gives it dignity.

The last stanza brings us from the wish of the poet back to her experience of the actual situation. This experience is condensed into the image 'Aber meine Schulter hängt herab / Von der Last des Flügels'. The angel is, in her poetry, like the star, a symbol of transcendence. It was through 'Flügelmenschen die des Wegs ein Stück / Mich meines Amtes wegen, stärken und begießen' that she came to understand her despair as a consequence of 'unerfüllte Gottesweisung', as we have seen earlier (see above, p. 55). The 'Last des Flügels' as a cipher for an unfulfilled spiritual task appears even more strongly in *Gebet*:

> Ich suche allerlanden eine Stadt,
> Die einen Engel vor der Pforte hat.
> Ich trage seinen großen Flügel
> Gebrochen schwer am Schulterblatt
> Und in der Stirne seinen Stern als Siegel.   (GW, I, 288)

It is out of this situation of frustration that the search for 'ewige, stille Hände' arises; 'ewige' perhaps implies once again that only her mother – who herself is often imagined as an angel ('War sie der große Engel / Der neben mir ging' GW, I, 169) – could meet this longing. The last line is a significant variation on the first: the substitution of 'mit meiner Heimat' for 'mit einem stillen Menschen' seems to hint that only in friendship a 'home' could be found.

But in her essay on friendship and love she goes even further. She sees in relationship a task to be fulfilled as an example for others:

> Jede Liebe, jede Freundschaft, die bestanden wird, dient zum
> Vorbild der Welt.   (GW, II, 612)

She seems to have had a gift for making friends, and also for antagonizing them. But whatever the fate of her relationships, some of her most successful poems are penetrating evocations of the personalities of her friends, most of them artists and writers. These poems are 'objective' in the sense discussed

earlier on; in them the poet's feelings about people she knew
and loved have crystallized into poetic portraits of great insight
and precision. Thus, a poem on Trakl starts with the lines:

> Seine Augen standen ganz fern.
> Er war als Knabe einmal schon im Himmel.
>
> Darum kamen seine Worte hervor
> Auf blauen und auf weißen Wolken.
>
> Wir stritten über Religion,
> Aber immer wie zwei Spielgefährten,
>
> Und bereiteten Gott von Mund zu Mund.   (GW, I, 256)

And a poem on Theodor Däubler starts:

> Zwischen dem Spalt seiner Augen
> Fließt dunkeler Golf.
>
> Auf seinen Schultern trägt er den Mond
> Durch die Wolken der Nacht.   (GW, I, 269)

Sometimes these poems contain elements of a very perceptive
kind of criticism, expressed with great originality. Thus for
instance, on Paul Zech:

> Paul Zech schreibt mit der Axt seine Verse.
>
> Man kann sie in die Hand nehmen,
> So hart sind die.   (GW, I, 252)

Or, less kindly, on Franz Werfel, in an otherwise affectionate
poem:

> Und fromm werden seine Lippen
> Im Gedicht.
>
> Manches trägt einen staubigen Turban,
> Er ist der Enkel seiner eigenen Verse.   (GW, I, 249)

In *Georg Grosz* she evokes most powerfully both the man and his
work. Lines like these make us see, and see with fresh eyes, this
artist's drawings:

> Seine Schrift regnet,
> Seine Zeichung: Trüber Buchstabe.
>
> Wie lange im Fluß gelegen,
> Blähen seine Menschen sich auf.

Mysteriöse Verlorene mit Quappenmäulern
Und verfaulten Seelen.

Fünf träumende Totenfahrer
Sind seine silbernen Finger.   (GW, I, 259)

In one of her best-known poems, *An meine Freunde*, a great deal
of what friendship meant to her is expressed. This is a complex
and in some ways elusive poem, but its wealth of 'outgoing'
impulses seems to me to make an attempt at a closer analysis
worth while:

Nicht die tote Ruhe –
Bin nach einer stillen Nacht schon ausgeruht.
Oh, ich atme Geschlafenes aus,
Den Mond noch wiegend
Zwischen meinen Lippen.

Nicht den Todesschlaf –
Schon im Gespräch mit euch
Himmlisch Konzert . . .
Und neu Leben anstimmt
In meinem Herzen.

Nicht der Überlebenden schwarzer Schritt!
Zertretene Schlummer zersplittern den Morgen.
Hinter Wolken verschleierte Sterne
Über Mittag versteckt –
So immer wieder neu uns finden.

In meinem Elternhause nun
Wohnt der Engel Gabriel . . .
Ich möchte innig dort mit euch
Selige Ruhe in einem Fest feiern –
Sich die Liebe mischt mit unserem Wort.

Aus mannigfaltigem Abschied
Steigen aneinandergeschmiegt die goldenen Staubfäden,
Und nicht ein Tag ungesüßt bleibt
Zwischen wehmütigem Kuß
Und Wiedersehn!

Nicht die tote Ruhe –
So ich liebe im Odem sein . . . !
Auf Erden mit euch im Himmel schon.
Allfarbig malen auf blauem Grund
Das ewige Leben.   (GW, I, 331–2)

This is the first version of this poem which appeared in Else Lasker-Schüler's last collection of poetry, *Mein blaues Klavier*. A second version, with some alterations, forms the end of a short prose essay, *Das heilige Abendmahl* (GW, II, 671–3), which is included in *Konzert*. This essay elaborates a rather daring comparison between the 'Tisch, um den Jesus von Nazareth mit den Jüngern das heilige Abendmahl feierte, seines Herzens über-flutende fromme Rose den Freunden reichte' and the table 'in einem verlorenen Winkel des Kaffeehauses' where the poet and her friends 'trank ein Meer des Trostes und zitternden Einsseins(. . .) in Gott'. The comparison may make us feel uneasy, but it shows something of the seriousness with which the poet regarded friendship, and of the transcendental value she attributed to it.

One of the clues to the meaning of the poem seems to me the contrast between two different kinds of sleep. This contrast is worked out in the first three stanzas: the first line of each rejects the 'tote Ruhe', that dead numbness for which we have seen the poet yearning in moments of despair. The remainder of the first two stanzas describe the state of being that follows a different kind of sleep, 'einer stillen Nacht', while the third stanza, on the other hand, conjures up the effects of the 'tote Ruhe' – these are again reversed in the last line by the hope of a new meeting.

Let us now inspect the individual stanzas more closely. The 'stille Nacht' of the first stanza need perhaps not be a night of sleep at all in the sense of a complete withdrawal from all aware-ness. What the poet seems to be striving to convey is an intimate communion with the night – here not a symbol of hostile chaos but of the unconscious as a source of life. This communion is expressed in physical terms: 'Geschlafenes' – perhaps dreams – is breathed out, and the moon is rocked like a baby between the poet's lips.

Stanza two: if death is seen as a return to 'paradise' – and we have seen that in moments of despair she was obsessed by this idea – it is not that paradise she is longing for here: the

'Himmlisch Konzert' is very much of this world, it is the life-giving talk with friends.

It is difficult not to associate with the first two lines of the next stanza the march of the Nazi jack-boots – the consequences of a 'Todesschlaf' are here given their most destructive expression. The thought of this stanza is not easy to follow, but I suggest this paraphrase: whatever survives 'Todesschlaf', a symbol for the life-denying withdrawal from contact, will destroy 'den Morgen', that is, life, hope and a new beginning. For it has trampled to death 'Schlummer' here set in contrast to 'Todesschlaf' and representing the other, life-giving kind of sleep. Then the stars – symbols for transcendence – remain covered until, again in a meeting with friends, the deadly spell is broken.

Stanza four shows how she imagines such a meeting – she sees it as a 'feast'. And where else could such a feast be celebrated but in the house of the parents, that mythical place of security, now, after her parents' death, transfigured by the presence of the Archangel Gabriel. This 'fixation' – if I may use a much abused word – on a paradisiacal childhood brings once more an element of fantasy into her very real wish for friendship and communication. At such a 'feast' there would be a fusion of friendship and love ('sich die Liebe mischt mit unserem Wort') which in her essay she describes as two separate states:

> Die Liebe ist ein Zustand, in den man durch himmlische Geschehnisse versetzt wird. (. . .) Die Freundschaft aber ist: von dieser Welt. (GW, II, 612)

But here, in the poem, the very act of communication is experienced as a state of love.

Stanza five is remarkable for its inclusion of separation and departure as part of the meeting between people. We have seen how often, with Else Lasker-Schüler, separation leads to despair, how the very fact of the impermanence of human relationship leads to a rejection of life. Here in a very compact and beautiful image, 'Abschied' itself becomes fruitful ground. The polarity of departure and 'Wiedersehn' is accepted.

The final stanza is a summary of the whole poem, and might be regarded as the poet's 'credo'. Here once more we find the rejection of dead numbness, and the praise of its opposite, 'Odem', breathing. (We are reminded of her story of the butterfly whom she brought back to life by breathing on it; see above, pp. 93–4.) 'Paradise' is not an ideal state, somewhere 'up there': it can be found on earth in contact with friends.

The last two lines sum up what communication means to her: it is a creative act, a painting embracing all colours, the totality of life, 'auf blauem Grund', that is, against the background of eternity.

(2) *The Erotic Encounter*

As we have seen, Else Lasker-Schüler distinguishes sharply in her essay *Freundschaft und Liebe* between the states of love and friendship. Highly though she values both, it appears that she considers love as a relationship on a higher plane. It is 'ein Zustand, in dem man durch himmlische Geschehnisse versetzt wird', while friendship is 'von dieser Welt' (GW, II, 612). At the same time, and just because it owes its origin to 'himmlische Geschehnisse', it seems a state beyond human endeavour and influence:

> An gemeinsamer Gefahr und am Spiel zweier Freunde stärkt sich die Freundschaft, aber nicht ein Jota mindert oder erhöht den Grad der Liebe jedwedes Bemühen. (*ibid.* p. 614)

The idea that one can be responsible for the development and growth of one's love seems alien to her. And this is perhaps one of the roots of her constant frustration and disappointment. Misfortune, like happiness, in love is outside human control:

> Wie aber erklärt man sich eine einseitige, sogenannte 'unglückliche' Liebe? Eine Liebe, die unerwidert bleibt. Vereitelt ein Unglücksfall, ein himmlischer natürlich, das hohe Geschehnis? (*ibid.* p. 613)

Mitteilung', communication, is a task for friends, not for lovers:

> Die Freunde müssen sich hörbarer mitteilen und sehnen sich täglich ähnlicher zu werden. Die Liebenden unähnlicher; gegenseitiges Bewundern; der Paragraph der Liebe! (*ibid.* p. 616)

The lovers' aim is not to talk but to look at each other in silent admiration. To make her meaning quite clear, she adds at this point two short poems, one addressed to the beloved and starting with the lines:

> Ich möchte ewig schweigen
> Einen Tod und ein Leben lang (. . .)   (GW, II, 616)

and another addressed to a friend which begins more colloquially:

> Ich möcht' mich unterhalten
> Mit dir von abends bis früh.   (*ibid.*)

We would hardly do justice to Else Lasker-Schüler, if we took the views expressed in this essay – or anywhere, for that matter – as something she clung to dogmatically. We have seen previously that she was well able to conceive of communication infused by love (see above, p. 101), but it is, I think, important to see that there was in her a tendency to see love as a heaven-sent state of being, infinitely desirable but entirely beyond one's control. Only by perceiving this tendency can we understand both the intensity of her longing, and the depth and frequency of her disappointment. It was, in a way, a child's attitude towards love.

I have called her longing for love the search for 'the erotic encounter' to indicate that this longing went far beyond mere sexual need. I propose, nevertheless, to examine first the way in which her attitude towards sex expressed itself in her poetry.

The Sexual Need

In his *Erinnerungen*, Sigismund von Radetzky quotes Else Lasker-Schüler as saying:

> Die körperliche Tat, aus der ein Mensch entsteht, ist etwas so Unmögliches, daß sie nur gerechtfertigt ist, wenn zwei vor lauter Liebe einfach nicht anders können.   (DD, p. 579)

The revulsion from the act of love-making which these words betray may have been a momentary reaction, and I have found nothing in her writing quite as extreme. But there are many signs of uneasiness about the physical aspect of love. In an essay, *Paradiese*, she has this to say about the nature of sexuality:

> Selbst die Dirne sehnt sich im Unterbewußtsein nach dem Paradiesüberbleibsel. Ihr Gewerbe ist nur Vorwand. Die Liebe ist immer ein psychischer Besitz, die Sexualität ihr Kelch. Die Sexualität zu verwerfen also, hieße den Leib nicht achten, der die Seele beherbergt. Irrig geschieht dies des öfteren. Aber zu verdammen dünkt mich die Sexualität, die nicht nach der Liebe Paradies sucht, ebenso der Körper, der seine Seele ungastlich birgt und verkommen läßt. (GW, II, 712)

This is a much more balanced view – until the word 'verdammen' breaks in explosively, like a messenger of fear and guilt. Later on, in the same essay, she says:

> Selbstverständlich gibt es eine Liebe, zubereitet im Liebeslichte Gottostens, die des Kelches nicht bedarf. (*ibid.*)

The love that does not need the 'vessel' of sexuality is clearly given pride of place, and this is perhaps an echo of those teachings of the Kabbalah which came close to a dualism that considered matter, and thus the body, as inferior. (We will have to consider later to what extent we can here speak of an 'influence of Jewish mysticism on Else Lasker-Schüler', or whether it would not be more correct to say that she was drawn to certain ideas in it towards which she in any case felt sympathetic (see below, pp. 129–33).)

It is interesting that in the following sentence she defines this love without sexuality as originating 'im Gespräch, das zum Konzert wird' (GW, II, 712). We are reminded of *An meine Freunde* where the 'Himmlisch Konzert', the talk with friends that is infused with love ('Sich die Liebe mischt mit unserem Wort'), is praised as the highest form of communication (see above, pp. 99–101). We meet here a strange ambiguity: on the one hand, love – heaven-sent, outside human control – is considered superior to any other kind of relationship. But when love implies physical union, it is the 'Gespräch mit euch' that is given greater value. This ambiguity seems to me characteristic of the

tension and anxiety with which the problem of human relationship is charged for this poet.

Most of the poems grappling with the feelings and sensations
of sexual need can be found in Else Lasker-Schüler's earliest
collection – they are, therefore, the work of a young woman.
But though they are, in many ways, immature, they often show
remarkable candour and insight. In some, the attempt is made
to express the sexual need as such: there is no partner. As an
example, I quote *Trieb*:

> Es treiben mich brennende Lebensgewalten,
> Gefühle, die ich nicht zügeln kann,
> Und Gedanken, die sich zur Form gestalten,
> Fallen mich wie Wölfe an!
>
> Ich irre durch duftende Sonnentage . . .
> Und die Nacht erschüttert von meinem Schrei.
> Meine Lust stöhnt wie eine Marterklage
> Und reißt sich von ihrer Fessel frei.
>
> Und schwebt auf zitternden, schimmernden Schwingen
> Dem sonn'gen Thal in den jungen Schoß,
> Und läßt sich von jedem Mai'nhauch bezwingen
> Und giebt der Natur sich willenlos.   (GW, I, 19)

A close analysis of this poem does not appear necessary. It
consists of a series of variations on one theme: the power and
blindness of the biological urge. At times over-dramatic ('Meine
Lust stöhnt wie eine Marterklage'), it is still a remarkable piece
of self-observation: the image concluding the first stanza gives
vivid expression to a psychological truth – the conversion of
unreleased sexual power into self-destructiveness. And the
last stanza, despite its more conventionally romantic imagery,
conveys with considerable conviction the lack of discrimination
in the sexual drive as long as it is undirected.

In *Trieb*, as in *Syrinxliedchen* (GW, I, 20) with its somewhat
obvious sexual symbolism ('Die Palmenblätter schnellen wie
Viperzungen / In die Kelche der roten Gladiolen'), the expression
of sexual need does not betray any feeling of guilt. Neither does
it in *Orgie* where the act of love-making is linked with those

fantasies of timelessness and paradise which we have encountered before as elements of de-realization and 'Verkindlichung':

> Der Abend küsste geheimnisvoll
> Die knospenden Oleander.
> Wir spielten und bauten Tempel Apoll
> Und taumelten sehnsuchtsübervoll
> Ineinander.
> Und der Nachthimmel goß seinen schwarzen Duft
> In die schwellenden Wellen der brütenden Luft,
> Und Jahrhunderte sanken
> Und reckten sich
> Und reihten sich wieder golden empor
> Zu sternenverschmiedeten Ranken.
> Wir spielten mit dem glücklichsten Glück,
> Mit den Früchten des Paradiesmai (. . .)   (GW, I, 28)

In this 'Golden Age' fantasy there is no place for the guilty entanglements of everyday life. As we have seen, it is in fact an escape from it. Sexual play is here an expression of childlike innocence. We met a very different view in *Der gefallene Engel*, where sexual involvement is seen as the 'fall' that causes the loss of 'paradise' (see above, pp. 62–3). Similarly, in *Sinnenrausch* the concepts of hell and sin are introduced:

> Dein sünd'ger Mund ist meine Totengruft,
> Betäubend ist sein süßer Atemduft,
> Denn meine Tugenden entschliefen.
> Ich trinke sinnberauscht aus seiner Quelle
> Und sinke willenlos in ihre Tiefen,
> Verklärten Blickes in die Hölle.   (GW, I, 31)

In *Fieber* too submission to the lover is felt as a kind of damnation:

> Ich weiß, ich bin verdammt
> Und fall aus Himmelshöhen in Deine Hände.   (GW, I, 29)

In *Sein Blut*, man's sexual need is seen as the destructive force – woman is here nothing but a helpless victim:

> Am liebsten griff er mein spielendes Herz
> Aus wiegendem Lenzhauch
> Und hing es auf wo an einem Dornstrauch.
> . . . Sein Blut plagt ihn.   (GW, I, 32)

These poems, though rich in telling imagery evoking the sultry climate of a strong but undirected sexuality, nevertheless lack balance and betray the poet's uneasiness by frequent melo-dramatic exaggeration. In a later poem, published in her second collection, she shows a considerably more differentiated feeling for the nature of physical desire, and a firmer grasp in conveying it:

> *O, meine schmerzliche Lust . . .*
>
> Mein Traum ist eine junge, wilde Weide
> Und schmachtet in der Dürre.
> Wie die Kleider um den Tag brennen . . .
> Alle Lande bäumen sich.
>
> Soll ich dich locken mit dem Liede der Lerche
> Oder soll ich dich rufen wie der Feldvogel?
> Tuuh! Tuuh!
>
> Wie die Silberähren
> Um meine Füße sieden – – –
> O, meine schmerzliche Lust
> Weint wie ein Kind. (GW, I, 145)

The first stanza finds very precise verbal equivalents for the physical sensation of unreleased desire. A paraphrase can only blur the contours where every word is apt. Once again, the strength of the stanza lies in the 'objectification' of an intensely subjective experience: the thirsty birch-tree is the 'objective correlative' for the poet's unfulfilled desire, the urge to shed the inhibiting, 'burning' clothes is projected on to the hot day, and the body's turmoil on to the landscape.

In the second stanza the poet re-enters, so to speak, the poem – but as a bird calling her mate. At the beginning of the last stanza, the sensation of inner heat is again expressed by a concrete external image which, by contrast, gives special poignancy to the naked personal outbreak at the end.

The Wish for Union

Rachel Katinka who knew Else Lasker-Schüler in Jerusalem wrote this of the poet, who was then seventy-one years old:

> Immer, immer war sie in jemanden verliebt, erwartete ihn, sehnte
> sich nach ihm, schmückte sich für ihn, schmückte das Zimmer zu
> seinem Empfang, war eifersüchtig und haßte die Frauen, die sie
> verdächtigte, daß sie sich ihr in den Weg stellen. (DD, p. 597)

One can find such behaviour in an old woman repulsive and
ridiculous – and some people have in fact found it so. And one
can also marvel at the wealth of her emotional resources, her
capacity for love – in whatever way one wishes to understand
this many-faceted word. Was her love always essentially self-
love, as Muschg suggests when he says: 'Im geliebten Du betet
sie im Grund sich selbst an'?[1] Or is she really concerned with
others, with contact, with relationship, as Max Fischer emphasized in his perceptive little essay:

> Es ist nicht zufällig, daß nicht nur jedes Buch, sondern auch
> jeder kleiner Essai, ja fast jedes einzelne Gedicht eine persönliche
> Widmung trägt – nur aus der Beziehung von Person zu Person
> quillt die Kraft dieses Schaffens, nur als Zeugnisse persönlicher
> Aussprache haben sie für die Dichterin Wert.[2]
>
> Immer ist es ihre Beziehung zu den Menschen, die im Mittelpunkt
> steht . . .[3]

Anyone who tries to gain a psychological perspective learns
before long that all either/or formulations are incomplete and
misleading, that the one *and* the other are always at work, that
opposites exclude each other only in the realm of logic. It is one
of the aims of this examination to show that it is, in Fischer's
words, 'die Beziehung zu den Menschen, die im Mittelpunkt
steht', but that this central concern for relationship went through
many stages of confusion, alienation and transformation. In
previous chapters our attention was focused on changes from the
wish for relatedness to the desolation of unrelatedness and self-
relatedness under the pressure of expectation and disappointment.
Now we shift the emphasis to moments when her wish for
union could unfold more freely, bringing forth a body of love

---

[1] Muschg, *op. cit.* p. 129.
[2] M. Fischer, 'Else Lasker-Schüler', *Das literarische Echo*, Berlin, 1918–19, p. 36.
[3] *Ibid.* p. 38.

poetry that is remarkable for its wealth, its variety of nuances and its power.

The scope of this love poetry is wide, ranging from simple love lyrics to complex 'metaphysical' speculations. All we can do in the context of this examination is to look at some poems and passages that embody particularly clearly certain significant aspects of her experience of love, bearing always in mind the contrapuntal nature of her poetry where several strands of melody often sound simultaneously, sometimes in 'Contrary motion', as the musician would say.

As an example of the numerous poems that celebrate the union with the beloved I quote *Ich liebe Dich*, which is remarkable for that sustained note of ecstatic simplicity of which she is sometimes capable:

> Ich liebe dich
> Und finde dich
> Wenn auch der Tag ganz dunkel wird.
>
> Mein Lebelang
> Und immer noch
> Bin suchend ich umhergeirrt.
>
> Ich liebe dich!
> Ich liebe dich!
> Ich liebe dich!
>
> Es öffnen deine Lippen sich . . .
> Die Welt ist taub,
> Die Welt ist blind
>
> Und auch die Wolke
> Und das Laub –
> – Nur wir, der goldene Staub
> Aus dem wir zwei bereitet:
> – Sind! (GW, I, 364)

The vocabulary of this poem is extremely simple, and there is a predominance of one-syllable words. The first four stanzas, formally and thematically, have the quality of a folk-song. It is a measure of the sincerity of the whole that the third stanza, with its threefold repetition of 'Ich liebe dich', comes off without jarring. The fifth stanza, formally more complex, brings also a greater complexity of thought: elaborating the preceding two lines, it denies existence to anything but the lovers – we remember Muschg's interpretation of 'golden' as a symbol of 'erotische Erfüllung' (see above, pp. 39–40). In giving 'sind' a line to itself, the poet emphasizes and draws together the meaning of the poem: love is the only true mode of 'being'.

A comparable simplicity can be found in *Melodie*:

> Deine Augen legen sich in meine Augen
> Und nie war mein Leben so in Banden,
> Nie hat es so tief in Dir gestanden
> Es so wehrlos tief.
>
> Und unter Deinen schattigen Träumen
> Trinkt mein Anemonenherz den Wind zur Nachtzeit,
> Und ich wandle blühend durch die Gärten
> Deiner stillen Einsamkeit.   (GW, I, 69)

The first stanza has, once more, a folk-song quality while the second shows traces of that metaphoric luxuriance which we have met as an aspect of Else Lasker-Schüler's tendency towards oriental embroidery. Here, however, it does not seem to me to break the mood – it is no more than a heightening of feeling. (A good example of the subtle balance, so easily overthrown, between the various elements that make a poem!)

More important is the appearance of a theme which, in its more destructive aspects, we have met, for instance, in *Hinter Bäumen berg ich mich* (see above, pp. 41–2) – the theme of the poet's dependence on her lover: her life is 'in Banden', it is 'wehrlos'. The existence of the beloved is expressed through the image of a garden on whose 'schattige Träume' and 'Wind zur Nachtzeit' the 'blossoming' of the poet depends. We have seen how this feeling of dependence can become the seed of disappointment and despair. Here it is still contained in the experience of union and contentment.

Thus it is in *Die Liebe* (GW, I, 116), where the lines 'Und ich werde heimwärts / Von deinem Atem getragen' link another image of utter reliance on the lover with the idea of 'home'.

The threat inherent in such reliance becomes more distinct in *An den Ritter* which starts with the lines

> Gar keine Sonne ist mehr,
> Aber dein Angesicht scheint (. . .)

and ends

> Wenn eine Wolke kommt –
> Sterbe ich.   (GW, I, 198)

Far removed from the simplicity and straightforward emotionality of those poems is the oriental baroque of that muchanthologized and frequently analysed poem *Ein alter Tibetteppich*:

> Deine Seele, die die meine liebet,
> Ist verwirkt mit ihr im Teppichtibet.
>
> Strahl in Strahl, verliebte Farben,
> Sterne, die sich himmellang umwarben.
>
> Unsere Füße ruhen auf der Kostbarkeit,
> Maschentausendabertausendweit.
>
> Süßer Lamasohn auf Moschuspflanzenthron,
> Wie lange küßt dein Mund den meinen wohl
> Und Wang die Wange buntgeknüpfte Zeiten schon?
>
>   (GW, I, 164)

Of this poem, Karl Kraus wrote enthusiastically in his *Fackel*, at the beginning of their friendship:

> Das hier . . . zitierte Gedicht gehört für mich zu den entzückendsten und ergreifendsten, die ich je gelesen habe, und wenige von Goethe abwärts gibt es, in denen so wie in diesem Tibetteppich Sinn und Klang, Wort und Bild, Sprache und Seele verwoben sind.[1]

A recent critic, Reinhold Grimm, who uses this poem as an illustration of what he calls 'konnektierende Lyrik', also stresses the cosmic unity embodied in these stanzas:

> Ding und Mensch, Zeit und Raum sind in diesen Versen zu einer einzigen großen Einheit geworden . . . Hier wird 'das Fest der glückhaften Vereinigung von Welt und Ich' (Höllerer) gefeiert.[2]

[1] *Die Fackel*, Nos. 313–14, 1910.
[2] R. Grimm, *Strukturen*, Göttingen, 1963, p. 185.

III

The lovers' union which is the poet's concern is here expressed on a number of planes simultaneously. It is the theme of the poem, stated by the first two lines: 'Deine Seele, die die meine liebet, / Ist verwirkt mit ihr im Teppichtibet'. It is embodied in the sustained 'conceit' of the carpet with its central idea of interweaving ('verwirkt', 'Strahl in Strahl', 'maschentausendabertausendweit', 'buntgeknüpfte Zeiten') – as Heselhaus puts it: 'Die Ich-und-Du-Beziehung ist im Teppich-Gewebe metaphorisiert'.[1] The idea of union is also expressed in structural details, through 'durchgängige Vertauschung im metaphorischen Schweben'.[2] Both Heselhaus and Grimm mention the word-play 'Tibetteppich – Teppichtibet' as an example of a 'Vertauschung der Bereiche',[3] Grimm points to 'buntgeknüpfte Zeiten' as an example of 'zeit-räumliche Verschränkung'.[4] Another structural embodiment of union is the neologism 'maschentausendabertausendweit' of which Grimm says that it could be part of 'einer holophrastischen Sprache', demonstrating the 'Intensität der Konnexion'.[5]

In the context of our examination, yet another question arises – that of the relation between reality and fantasy. The change from 'Tibetteppich' to 'Teppichtibet' is, as Heselhaus already indicates, the dissolution of a concrete symbol for union, the carpet, into the imaginary Tibet of the Carpets, 'ein Traumland von Teppichwundern'.[6] Similarly, the beloved appears at the end of the poem in the 'mask' of the 'Lamasohn auf Moschuspflanzenthron'. Do we meet here, as we did before, a process of fantastication as a sign of escape from naked reality?

A similar question is posed by the following poem:

Ein Liebeslied

Komm zu mir in der Nacht – wir schlafen engverschlungen.
Müde bin ich sehr, vom Wachen einsam.
Ein fremder Vogel hat in dunkler Frühe schon gesungen,
Als noch mein Traum mit sich und mir gerungen.

---

[1] Heselhaus, *op. cit.* pp. 215–16.   [2] *Ibid.*
[3] Grimm, *op. cit.* p. 185.   [4] *Ibid.*   [5] *Ibid.*
[6] Heselhaus, *op. cit.* p. 216.

Es öffnen Blumen sich vor allen Quellen
Und färben sich mit deiner Augen Immortellen . . .

Komm zu mir in der Nacht auf Siebensternenschuhen
Und Liebe eingehüllt spät in mein Zelt.
Es steigen Monde aus verstaubten Himmelstruhen.

Wir wollen wie zwei seltene Tiere liebesruhen
Im hohen Rohre hinter dieser Welt.   (GW, I, 361)

The *Tibetteppich* glorifies a state of union which has actually
come about, which is present – though we felt we had to ask
whether the manner of its glorification does not draw a veil of
fantasy over this here-and-now reality. *Ein Liebeslied*, on the
other hand, is a call for union. It opens in great simplicity, not
unlike *Ich liebe Dich* and *Melodie* (see above, pp. 109–10). A number of key-words build up the loneliness out of which the call for
union breaks forth – 'müde', 'einsam', 'fremder Vogel', 'dunkle
Frühe'. The next stanza sustains this note, but in the third, with
'Siebensternenschuhen', there is a change of tone. Once more
an oriental setting is implied – 'Komm zu mir (. . .) in mein Zelt'.
The question is once again: does here an oriental costume hide
the naked body of experience, or has the poet found the true
metaphoric embodiment of her feeling? It is a question which in
the individual instant will be answered differently by different
readers, but it cannot be ignored when considering the work of
a poet who – as we have seen – holds such a precarious position
between rejection of what *is* and going out towards it. For
myself, the 'Siebensternenschuhe' and the invitation into the
tent strike me as a blurring of the experiential truth expressed
before. I feel differently about the next line which, though a
fantastic image, seems to me to offer a valid objectification of a
very personal experience: the 'illumination' of the night of
loneliness and sterility (this latter idea seems implied by the
epithet 'verstaubt') by the arrival of the lover. This seems to me
even more true of the last two lines. One might perhaps object
to 'seltene Tiere' as introducing a touch of preciousness, but
I feel that the state the poet describes is rare enough to warrant
this metaphor. These seem to me among the most beautiful lines

Else Lasker-Schüler wrote, deeply felt and expressing with great precision the state of 'liebesruhen' – the mysterious stillness of the union of lovers, which is, at the same time, in and beyond nature.

The theme of union includes its opposite, separation. In the first part of our examination we found that it was separation from the beloved that frequently leads to resentment, despair and withdrawal. Absolute demand turns into absolute rejection. Personal disappointment is experienced as a catastrophe of cosmic dimensions. But this is not always so. At times, the love impulse is strong and 'outgoing' enough to bear the separation. Then sadness takes the place of despair, and hope is not destroyed by absence. Sadness predominates in *In meinem Schoße*:

> In meinem Schoße
> Schlafen die dunkelen Wolken –
> Darum bin ich so traurig, du Holdester. (GW, I, 365)

But union is not entirely destroyed:

> Es rauscht der Flügel des Geiers
> Und trägt mich durch die Lüfte
> Bis über dein Haus. (*ibid.*)

Hope remains alive:

> Lösche mein Herz nicht aus –
> Du den Weg findest –
> Immerdar. (*ibid.*)

This, like *Ich liebe Dich*, is one of the poet's late love poems and has the touching simplicity of many of these. That they were written by a woman of seventy is astonishing but does not, to my mind, impair their quality. And they do not seem to support Muschg's suggestion that all her love was essentially self-love (see above, p. 108). Perhaps it would be possible to say that *In meinem Schoße* shows a touch of resignation that betrays the age of the writer. An earlier poem, *Ein Lied der Liebe*, dealing with the same theme, lacks this element. It is a joyful affirmation of union in spite of external separation. I quote some relevant lines:

Seit du nicht da bist
Ist die Stadt dunkel. (. . .)
Du liebst mich wieder –
Wem soll ich mein Entzücken sagen? (. . .)
Ich weiß immer,
Wann du an mich denkst –
Dann wird mein Herz ein Kind
Und schreit. (. . .)
Wenn doch ein Tiger
Seinen Leib streckte
Über die Ferne, die uns trennt,
Wie zu einem nahen Stern.

Auf meinem Angesicht
Liegt früh dein Hauch.   (GW, I, 184–5)

Among the poems which show her 'outgoing' erotic impulse,
I would also count those where she expresses a genuine concern
for a lover whose love she can no longer return. This may seem
paradoxical, unless one is ready to use 'erotic' in its widest sense:
as concern for the other one, the wish for human communion.
This we find in *Dir*:

Drum wein' ich
Daß bei Deinem Kuß
Ich so nichts empfinde
Und ins Leere versinken muß.
      Tausend Abgründe
Sind nicht so tief,
Wie diese große Leere.
Ich sinne im engsten Dunkel der Nacht,
      Wie ich Dir's ganz leise sage,
Doch ich habe nicht den Mut.
Ich wollte, es käme ein Südenwind,
Der Dir's herüber trage,
Damit es nicht gar voll Kälte kläng'
Und er Dir's warm in die Seele säng'
      Kaum merklich durch Dein Blut.   (GW, I, 61)

The very acknowledgement of her own inability to respond, of
her emptiness and coldness, seems already a bridge over the gulf

of separation. Is the fact that she can feel nothing of her lover's kisses not almost outweighed by the care and tenderness with which she considers a way of making her confession 'ganz leise', and 'Damit es nicht gar voll Kälte kläng''? A love relationship has come to an end – but does it not almost sound as if another kind of relationship was about to begin?

A similar tender concern for the suffering of the other is expressed in the first stanza of *Schuld*:

> Als wir uns gestern gegenübersassen,
> Erschrak ich über deine Blässe,
> Über die Leidenslinie Deiner Wange,
> Da kam's, daß meine Gedanken mich vergassen
> Über der Leidenslinie Deiner Wange. (GW, I, 63)

The last two lines are a simple and infinitely moving description of an important experience which is rare in all of us: in being entirely with another person, our 'thoughts forget us', our self-involvement ceases. In this poem, however, the moment of meeting passes without bearing fruit: in the second stanza the guilt over her inability to respond to the lover's request destroys the bridge which concern has just built:

> Dumpf läutete noch einmal Brand mein Leben
> Und schrumpfte dann zusammen wie ein Blatt. (GW, I, 63)

Once again, the poet expresses intuitively a deep psychological truth. By the use of the words 'schrumpfte (. . .) zusammen', she conveys very accurately the crippling force of guilt that makes us 'shrink' into a state of non-existence where any basis for meeting and union has disappeared.

There is yet another aspect of the lovers' union that finds expression in her love poetry – an aspect that lights up momentarily in the second stanza of *Liebesflug*:

> Und wir griffen unsere Hände,
> Die verlöteten wie Ringe sich;
> Und er sprang mit mir auf die Lüfte
> Gotthin, bis der Atem verstrich. (GW, I, 114)

The key-word is 'gotthin' – it shows the direction into which the poet's longing for union ultimately points: towards God. At this moment, the I–Thou relationship of lover and beloved becomes transparent to the encounter with 'the Being that is directly, most nearly and lastingly, over against us, that may properly only be addressed not expressed', as Buber puts it.[1] A similar break-through into another dimension occurs in the second stanza of *Unser Liebeslied*:

> Und wir wollen unter Pinien
> Heimlich beide umschlungen gehn,
> In die blaue Allmacht sehn.   (GW, I, 123)

Instead of the stormy movement of *Liebesflug* we have here the still contemplation of the Eternal – 'blue' is once more the 'Gottesfarbe' (see above, pp. 49 and 102) – emerging from the peace of loving closeness. We have thus reached the point where her unceasing wish for contact, communication and union becomes finally a religious concern, a longing for the Eternal Thou.

(3) *The Search for God*

In the previous chapter, our tracing of the forward movement of Else Lasker-Schüler's existential 'pendulum' took us to the point where her longing for contact turns into a search for God. Her 'Liebesflug' carries her 'gotthin', and a loving embrace leads to a contemplation of the 'blaue Allmacht' (see above). But already our outline of the backward swing into despair and isolation touched frequently on the border behind which an image of God became visible. Sometimes it was a God who had withdrawn from his creation (see above, p. 46), at other times it was a God very much present to be questioned, even if he did not answer (see above, pp. 47 and 72). We have met the 'Verkindlichung' of the image of God as an aspect of the poet's escape from the pain of reality into a paradise of fantasy (see above, pp. 59–60 and 72). And we have also found her mourning

---

[1] M. Buber, *I and Thou*, New York, 1958, p. 80.

for God's death (see above, p. 84), a feeling very far removed from any facile atheism – for how could one talk about the 'grave' of someone who had never existed?

But it is the forward swing of the pendulum, it is her deep concern for loving communication, for contact with the other one, that compelled her to seek out a Thou transcending all other thous. In this search, the pendulum reaches its furthest forward point. It is at this point also that this metaphorical pendulum, unlike its physical brother, comes to rest, reconciling in some rare moments all opposing movements.

Martin Buber has called it 'the greatest achievement of Israel' that it 'has taught men that they can address this God in very reality, that men can say Thou to Him'.[1] In this sense, Else Lasker-Schüler was certainly a truly Jewish poet. In what other ways did she reflect her Jewish background?

The Importance of Judaism

She was always proudly conscious of being a Jew. Throughout her essays and letters we find references to what her Jewish origin and the Jewish faith meant to her. Thus she writes in an essay describing the practice and meaning of the highest Jewish feast, the Day of Atonement:

> Es ist schön, Jude zu sein, ist man ihm nie aus dem Weg gegangen, um eher das Ziel zu erreichen, ist man ihm treu geblieben und mit ihm verwachsen, von keiner äußeren Nichtigkeit verführt, aber vom Jordan umspült. Wer vermag mich zu entreißen dem uralten Jehovagebein, dem unerschütterlichen Fels! (GW, II, 750)

The last sentence of this quotation is taken up in one of her best-known poems, *Mein Volk*, but in a context that not only stresses the deep bond between her and her people, but also the way in which she felt this bond to be threatened:

> Der Fels wird morsch,
> Dem ich entspringe
> Und meine Gotteslieder singe . . .
> Jäh stürz ich vom Weg

M. Buber, *Hasidism*, New York, 1948, p. 96.

Und riesele ganz in mir
Fernab, allein über Klagegestein
Dem Meer zu.

Hab mich so abgeströmt
Von meines Blutes
Mostvergorenheit.
Und, immer, immer noch der Widerhall
In mir,
Wenn schauerlich gen Ost
Das morsche Felsgebein,
Mein Volk,
Zu Gott schreit.   (GW, I, 137)

The first stanza of this poem shows both the poet's connection
with the 'Fels', and her separation from it. The 'Fels' is here no
longer 'unerschütterlich' as in the earlier quotation – it has
become 'morsch'. The poem itself does not say why she thinks
of the ancient Jewish 'rock' as crumbling, but we know from other
sources that she was by no means uncritical of Jewish life in
modern times, particularly in Palestine. Catherine Küster-
Ginsberg throws some light on the poet's complex attitude:

> Der Jude war ihr Problem, ihm galt ihre übersteigende Liebe.
> Mit ihm hatte sie zu dichten begonnen, er kehrte in jedem
> Gespräch zurück. Ihre Juden waren biblische Gestalten, Seher,
> Dichter, Weise. Wie konnte sie sich mit der Realität befreunden?
> Sie suchte Aufbau im Geistigen, und nahm es dem palestinensi-
> schen Juden übel, daß er mit seinem Kampf um Erde und Leben
> 'zu fest auf zwei Beinen stand'. Wenn sie verletzt von der
> Unvollkommenheit, vom Ungeist, auf Beziehungslosigkeit
> stieß, brach sie aus: 'Das sind gar keine richtigen Juden. Wir
> müssen das Wort Jude abschaffen, Hebräer sollen sie werden!'[1]

A similar point is made by S. von Radetzky when he writes:

> Sie liebte nicht die jüdischen Anekdoten. Diese erschienen ihr eine
> Banalisierung des Judentums. Ihre Vorstellung vom Gottesvolke
> hatte etwas Makkabäisches – 'die wilden Juden'.   (DD, pp. 578–9)

The first line of *Mein Volk* points perhaps at this 'Banalisierung
des Judentums' which had removed the Jewish people so far

---

[1] K. Küster, *op. cit.*

away from the 'biblische Gestalten' to whom the poet was so deeply devoted. All the same: this is the 'rock' where she had her origin, and it is this origin which enables her to sing her 'songs of God'. How much she regarded her poetry as essentially Jewish is shown by her reply to a suggestion that they should be translated into Hebrew: 'Aber sie sind doch hebräisch geschrieben!' (DD, p. 598). And we have reason to believe that by 'Gotteslieder' she did not only mean her explicitly religious poems: just as she saw the ancient prophets as poets, she thought of the poet's task as essentially prophetic, a 'Platz machen für Gott!' (GW, II, 697).

The second part of the stanza continues the metaphor of the stream which having originated in the rock now pursues its lonely course towards the sea. This separation from her origin is a source of regret for the poet, her way leads 'über Klage-gestein'. And I do not think that she holds the 'decay' of the 'rock' alone responsible for it: she herself has lost contact with her Jewish background. This separation is also expressed by the image which opens the second stanza: as the colourless serum separates from the blood cells after coagulation, she has split herself off from the 'blood' of her people which is nevertheless her own blood. But the echo of her people's cries to God continues to reverberate in her.

I cannot altogether agree with Heselhaus' analysis of this poem:

> Man kann annehmen, daß die Bildvorstellung von Fels . . . der Bibelsprache entlehnt ist. Ich erinnere etwa Jesaia 51, 1 'Schauet den Fels an, davon ihr gehauen seid, und des Brunnens Gruft, daraus ihr getragen seid.' . . . Die Fels-Metapher im Gedicht schwankt zwischen Gott und Judenvolk: denn anfangs singt sie dem Felsen Gotteslieder, und am Ende ist das morsche Felsgebein ihr Volk. Zwischen beiden Bedeutungen ist eine Bewegung, die von Gott wegströmt und zu Gott zurückschreit . . . aufgefangen: im ersten Teil ein deutendes Bild vom eigenen Weg über Klage-gestein zum Meer; im zweiten Teil ein unmittelbares Lebensbe-kenntnis, das Bild vom Wasserlauf auf das Blut übertragend und damit auch das Schicksal ihres Volkes übernehmend.[1]

---

[1] Heselhaus, *op. cit.* p. 225.

Heselhaus' reference to the Isaiah passage is useful. But I do not think that the 'Fels-Metapher . . . schwankt zwischen Gott und Judenvolk' – I see no reason to assume that 'Fels' does not stand both in the beginning and at the end for 'Volk'. When Heselhaus says that the poet in this poem takes on the destiny of her people, this does not seem to me altogether precise: *Mein Volk* exhibits an ambivalent attitude embracing both identification and separation. The identification with the fate of her people comes out more clearly at other times, as when she writes:

> Mein Heimatmeer lauscht still in meinem Schoß,
> Helles Schlafen – dunkles Wachen . . .
> In meiner Hand liegt schwer mein Volk begraben (. . .)
>
> (GW, I, 144)

Or, in a poem published posthumously:

> Ein einziger Mensch ist oft ein ganzes Volk (. . .)
>
> (GW, III, 113)

A similar identification, but this time experienced as a burden, occurs in *Ewige Nächte*. This is a poem of isolation and despair: the poet sits at her table, looking at a 'scar' in it, and her wish to throw off the burden of consciousness concretizes itself in the vision of a primitive man whose knife perhaps once gave a tree this 'scar':

> Vielleicht stieß mal ein Messer in den Stamm
> Ein Mann im Walde, – seine Lust zu kühlen.
> Und reckte weit am Teiche in den Schlamm
> Die Glieder, die entlasteten zu fühlen.
>
> Er warf mit seinem Tropfen letzter Lust
> Die Menschheit von sich ab in einer einzigen Wehe.
> Ich wälze auch, wie er, mein 'Ich' bewußt!
> Ein Volk von mir, bevor ich aus dem Leben gehe.
>
> (GW, I, 325)

These are only two stanzas of a long and difficult poem, and even these I do not propose to analyse in detail. In our context it is sufficient to look at the last two lines. They too are not easy to grasp, though their obscurity is mainly due to the eccentric

punctuation. Either 'mein "Ich" bewußt!' and 'Ein Volk' are both
the direct object of 'Ich wälze' – the meaning would then be:
like this primitive man, I throw my Ego *and* my people off
before I part from life. Or else, 'mein "Ich" bewusst!' is in apposi-
tion to 'Ich wälze' – then it would mean: I also, conscious of
my Ego, throw my people off before I part from life. In any case,
the essential point of these lines is the deep connection the poet
felt to exist between the destiny of her people and herself.

The Bible

We have seen (see above, p. 119) that one of Else Lasker-
Schüler's main difficulties in coming to terms with the reality
of modern Judaism was her attachment to the figures of the
Bible: 'Ihre Juden waren biblische Gestalten, Seher, Dichter,
Weise.' In the essay *Meine Andacht* she expressed her feelings
about the scriptures:

> Jahre las ich die Abende einsam in den Büchern, die im Jenseits
> gedruckt wurden. Nicht wie man Reihe auf Reihe zu lesen pflegt,
> aber über Wege schreitend mit den Menschen der Urerzählungen,
> die die Wurzel legten zur Menschheit. Wer *so* den Stoff der
> Testamente zu sich nimmt, der hat vom Brot des Lebens gegessen.
>
> (GW, II, 740)

The influence of the Bible on her is strong, and can be seen
both in her choice of themes and in her style. Though a discussion of her style would go beyond the context of our enquiry,
I would like to make a few comments on K. J. Höltgen's detailed
analysis of what he calls this poet's 'orientalische Gestaltungs-
prinzipien'.[1] It is certainly true that the paratactic structure and
hyperbolic imagery of a great deal of her poetry reminds us of
the language of the Bible, but to what extent these stylistic
elements can be derived entirely from the poet's Jewish background remains at least questionable. Höltgen suggests 'ererbte
jüdische Geistesanlage' and 'Aufwachsen in jüdischer literari-
scher Tradition'[2] as sources for the poet's 'orientalische Meta-
phorik'. But is not the concept of an 'ererbte jüdische Geistes-

[1] Höltgen, *op. cit.* pp. 38ff. [2] Höltgen, *op. cit.* p. 54

anlage' – at another point Höltgen speaks of 'Urerinnerung orientalischer Lyrik'[1] – too vague and nebulous as an explanation of certain concrete forms of structure and imagery? And as far as Jewish literary tradition is concerned, we do not really know how great a part this played in her life – all we do know is that she loved the Bible and probably read some versions of Kabbalistic teaching.

The problem of her style seems to me extremely complex and in need of further thorough investigation. I think that any such investigation would have to take into account the nature of modern poetry as such. Beside Höltgen's statement that her early poems

> erwecken meist den Eindruck einer bunten Perlenschnur aneinandergereihter Bilder. In parataktischer Fügung, nur selten durch Konjunktionen verbunden, entwickeln je zwei oder drei Verszeilen ein Bild oder einen Gedanken . . .[2]

– characteristics which he sees as essentially oriental – one would have to put, for instance, Hugo Friedrich's remarks on discontinuity as a characteristic of modern poetry:

> Diskontinuität statt Verbindung, Nebeneinandersetzung statt Fügung: das sind die Stilzeichen einer inneren Diskontinuität, eines Sprechen an der Grenze des Unmöglichen.[3]

I think that it is this 'Sprechen an der Grenze des Unmöglichen' that is often responsible for the 'parataktische Fügung' of Else Lasker-Schüler's poetry, rather than any 'Urerinnerung orientalischer Lyrik'.

In saying this, I do not by any means wish to deny the influence of the Bible on her work. Where this influence is well integrated, where the biblical diction is no mere ornamentation and the biblical figures are no mere 'masks', the result is impressive. This integration is found most frequently in the *Hebräische Balladen*. We have already spoken about the greater degree of 'objectification' of personal experience found in most of these (see above,

[1] *Ibid.* p. 34. [2] *Ibid.* p. 33.
[3] H. Friedrich, *Die Struktur der modernen Lyrik*, Hamburg, 1956, p. 89.

pp. 58 and 78–80), and this plays a major part in making this perhaps the most evenly excellent of all her collections.

F. A. Meyer quotes Arnold Zweig as saying – in an article celebrating Else Lasker-Schüler's 50th birthday in 1926 – that 'die Gestalten der Bibel . . . in ihrer Unmittelbarkeit seit Rembrandt nicht mehr so angeschaut worden seien wie von den Augen dieser Frau'.[1] To this immediacy of vision one would like to add the striking originality of her interpretation of biblical events already stressed by Wiener in his otherwise not very sympathetic essay:

> Biblischer Geist nach eigenem Bilde umgeschmiedet. Von allem Vertrauten wird abgesehen, auch vom üblichen Wesentlichen nur gewisse unerwartete, nur gefühlsmäßige Momente, die Rückschlüsse auf Seelisches veranlassen, werden hervorgehoben. Eigen ungeformte biblische Gestalten werden zeitlose Symbole, allem zufällig Individuellen enthoben.[1]

Let us look, for instance, at the poem called *Jakob*:

> Jakob war der Büffel seiner Herde.
> Wenn er stampfte mit den Hufen,
> Sprühte unter ihm die Erde.
>
> Brüllend ließ er die gescheckten Brüder.
> Rannte in den Urwald an die Flüsse,
> Stillte dort das Blut der Affenbisse.
>
> Durch die müden Schmerzen in den Knöcheln
> Sank er vor dem Himmel fiebernd nieder,
> Und sein Ochsgesicht erschuf das Lächeln.   (GW, I, 297)

At first sight, this seems to have very little to do with the biblical Jacob. The landscape is exotic – we see a herd of cattle moving through the jungle, Jacob is its leader. Then it seems he is attacked by monkeys and runs to the river to still the bleeding from his wounds. What are we to make of this? There is something pagan about it, and she does, in fact, write about this poem: 'Im Rausch der Dichtung wird wohl jeder Dichter einmal zum Heiden – auch ich, als ich mein Gedicht "Jakob" dichtete' (GW, II, 781). But in the same essay, she also writes about the

---

[1] *Op. cit.* p. 187.

difficulty transition from the worship of animal idols to the adoration of the one invisible God, a transition which Israel accomplished and by which it distinguished itself from other people. Something of the process of this transition is expressed in *Jakob*. Jacob is still animal-man, primitive, wild. But, as the last stanza describes, through suffering, through pain he comes to a realization of another dimension of being, a realization that literally forces him to his knees. The ox, the animal, 'creates' that most human of all expressions, the smile. Animal man becomes human through leaving the collective (the 'herd'), suffering pain, recognizing his limitation. The poet has commented on this last, mysteriously beautiful line:

> Es steht in der Kabbala . . . 'Wenn der Stier lächelt, wird das Lamm geboren.' Diese Offenbarung vergewaltigte mich in Vers. Eitelkeit kommt hier nicht in Frage, und ich beteure, nie im Leben vor meiner hebräischen Ballade 'Jakob' je in der Kabbala gelesen zu haben, noch von ihrem Inhalt gewußt durch Hörensagen. Ich beuge mich demütig vor meiner heiligen Erleuchtung. (GW, II, 782)

Whether she had really not heard of the Kabbalistic saying before writing the poem, or whether it did, in fact, prompt her, perhaps without her knowing it, to write the line, does not matter. The quotation confirms our interpretation by taking it one step further: the smile, one of the earliest of human expressions, leads to the birth of the lamb, the sacrificial animal, a symbol of Christ who is both God and man.

A similar re-interpretation is offered by the poem *Abraham und Isaak*. Abraham is described as the friend of the angels who 'ruhten gern vor seiner frommen Hütte / Und Abraham erkannte jeden' (GW, I, 294). But this idyllic situation is suddenly disturbed:

> Bis sie dann einmal bang in ihren Träumen
> Meckern hörten die gequälten Böcke,
> Mit denen Isaak Opfern spielte hinter Süßholzbäumen. (*ibid.*)

God's demand for the sacrifice of Isaac seems to follow from there. Is this then to be understood as a simple act of retribution – Isaac has 'played sacrifice' with the rams, and therefore has now to be sacrified in turn? I do not think that such a crude explanation of the old story is in the poet's mind. Isaac torturing the rams behind the 'liquorice trees' while Abraham is holding friendly intercourse with the angels outside his hut – this strikes me as a vivid symbol of the ambiguity of human nature where spiritual aspiration and instinctual cruelty may exist side by side. It is as an atonement of this situation, I think, that Isaac's sacrifice is here demanded, though – as in the story itself – God does not insist on its execution.

But it is not only in the creative re-telling of the old stories that the impact of the Bible on Else Lasker-Schüler's poetry shows itself. There are some biblical themes that expressed specific concerns of hers, and that appear frequently in her work. Among these themes the idea of the Fall has a special place. We have already seen that Else Lasker-Schüler was haunted by the image of a lost paradise (see above, p. 59), a state of idyllic harmony beyond good and evil, which she associated with childhood and which her fantasy furnished as a kind of retreat from painful reality. In some of her poems, however, she concerned herself with the antithesis Paradise–Fall not so much as a pretext for a glorification of regression and flight, but as a basic symbol for an inner conflict, for her struggle for acceptance. *Genesis* may serve as an example:

> Aus Algenmoos und Muscheln schleichen feuchte Düfte . . .
> Frohlockend schmiegt die Erde ihren Arm um meine Hüfte.
> – Mein Geist hat nach dem Heiligen Geist gesucht – .
>
> Und tauchte auf den Vogelgrund der Lüfte
> Und grub nach Gott in jedem Stein der Klüfte
> Und blieb doch Fleisch, leibeigen und verflucht.
>
> Ich keimte schon am Zweig der Liebesgifte,
> Als noch der Schöpfer durch die Meere schiffte,
> Das Wasser trennte von der Bucht.
>
> Und alles gut fand, da Er seine Erde prüfte,
> Und nicht ein Korn sprießt ungebucht.
>
> Doch seine beiden Menschen trieb Er in die Flucht!
> Noch schlief der Weltenplan in Seinem Schöpferstife.
> Sie fügten sich nicht Seiner väterlichen Zucht.

Unbändig wie das Feuer zwischen Stein und Stein
Noch ungeläutert zu entladen sich versucht,
So trotzten sie!!
Wie meines Herzens ungezäumte Wucht. (GW, I, 326)

In this poem, two threads are interwoven: a re-telling of the biblical account of Creation and Fall, and the poet's own 'fall'. The difference between *Genesis* and, say, *Abraham und Isaak* is that the poet here does not allow the story to represent her problem – she enters the poem herself. We are, thus, asked to feel ourselves into a situation where the poet is actually present while the world is in the process of being created, and this is not altogether easy. If, however, we are ready to accept this assumption, the development of the poem becomes fairly clear.

The first line presents an image of the world still in a state of chaos, the second switches over to a metaphor conjuring up a complete union of the 'I', the poet, with the rest of creation. In the beginning there was no division, man and universe were one. But the third line already introduces the element of separation: it is the very search of the human spirit for the 'Holy Ghost', the divine creative principle, that dissolves its one-ness with the universe and leads to the realization of its limitations ('Und blieb doch Fleisch, leibeigen und verflucht'). Even before the creation was completed, stanzas three and four maintain, the seed of the fall was present in man. This telescoping of events which in the Bible follow each other – creation and fall – gives a true picture of man's inner situation where indeed the opposites, creation and destruction, one-ness and division, always exist side by side. Another kind of telescoping leads to the line 'Ich keimte schon am Zweig der Liebesgifte' – if by 'Liebesgift' the apple is meant that led to the fall: the poet identifies both with the instrument of the fall and with tempted, and ultimately fallen man. Again, the simultaneity of inner events are, so to speak, contrapuntally expressed – a possibility that is specific to poetry.

In the remaining two stanzas the angle of vision shifts. The poet disappears from the scene that is now dominated by the fate of Adam and Eve. By expressing the flame of their rebellion through the image of early fire-making, Adam and Eve are presented implicitly as primitive men who in promethean mastery forget the Divine authority beyond them. In the last line the poet refers once again to herself: but this time she does not enter the scene, but only compares her heart's 'violence' with the rebellion of Adam and Eve.

It is important to note that the instrument of temptation, in *Genesis*, is called 'Liebesgift'. When looking at *Der gefallene Engel*, we have already observed that for Else Lasker-Schüler the 'fall' from innocence, the expulsion from paradise, was associated with sexual involvement (see above, pp. 62–3) – in this she concurred with the popular belief that the 'original sin' was sexual in nature, but also with those aspects of Jewish mysticism that, as we shall see, tend to present the physical aspect of life as inferior and corrupting (see below, pp. 132–3). The 'fall' from sexual innocence into erotic despair seems to me also the theme of that strange, turbulent and obscure poem *Erkenntnis* and its second simplified version *Die Stimme Edens* (GW, I, 111 and 156). The poet's mouthpiece here is the biblical Eve who after the 'Tag, den du Gott abrangst, / Da du zu früh das Licht sahst / Und in den blinden Kelch der Scham sankst' is expelled from paradise by guilt and anxiety:

> Deine Angst rollt über die Erdstufen
> Den Rücken Gottes herab.   (GW, I, 157)

The sexual nature of her 'Scham' is less clear in the second than in the first version of the poem which opens with these lines, later omitted:

> Schwere steigt aus allen Erden auf
> Und wir ersticken im Bleidunst,
> Jedoch die Sehnsucht reckt sich
> Und speit wie eine Feuersbrunst.
> Es tönt aus allen wilden Flüssen
> Das Urgeschrei, Evas Lied.
> Wir reißen uns die Hüllen ab,
> Vom Schall der Vorwelt hingerissen,
> Ich nackt! Du nackt!   (GW, I, 111)

Among the poems published after her death there are some poetic fragments which show the impact of the Bible in a very different way. These were probably written towards the end of her life, and like many of her late poems they have a new simplicity and directness. Here something nearer to the orthodox core of the Jewish faith, far removed from the subtleties and ambiguities of mysticism, breaks through. Thus, for instance, the following lines that have the message of the first commandment at their centre:

> Ein Feuer ging aus vom Ewigen.
> Gott ist und keine Götter sind neben ihm.
> Er weiß um das Verborgene und um das Offenbare.
> Er ist voller Güte und Mitleid.   (GW, III, 9)

Similarly, the following three lines celebrating the eve of the Sabbath, one of Judaism's great feasts:

> Am Freitagabend brennt das Licht
> Und welches aufsteigt in die Himmel
> Gott übersieht die kleinste Kerze nicht.   (GW, III, 111)

And another fragment on the same subject:

> Ich falte meine Hände in der Abendstunde
> Und auch dasselbe höre ich aus aller Juden Judenmunde
> Die wir am Freitagabend knieen vor den Kerzen:
> Erbarm dich, lieber Vater, und erweiche ihre Herzen.
> Mein Leib und meine Seele sollen weiter fasten.   (GW, III, 112)

Affinity with Jewish Mysticism

But it is only rarely, and only at the end of her life, that the poet reached such straightforwardness. Most of the time, her approach to religion showed a marked affinity with the complexities of Jewish mysticism.

I find it fitting to speak here of 'affinity' rather than 'influence'. Though S. von Radetzky says that 'sie las immer wieder die Kabbala' (DD, p. 580), we have reason to believe that Gehlhoff-Claes' more precise comment – in a note on one of the poet's

letters to Kraus in which she refers to reincarnation – comes
nearer the truth:

> Hier und im folgenden Anspielungen auf Gedanken der kabba-
> listischen Lehre, mit der die Dichterin sich zwar nicht systematisch,
> aber gelegentlich auseinandersetzte und deren Zeichen in der
> Dichtung wie in der persönlichen Gedankenwelt zu finden sind.
>
> (BK, p. 122)

We have no reason to believe that Else Lasker-Schüler was a
systematic student of the various complicated doctrines of
Jewish mysticism. I doubt, in fact, whether it was in her nature
to be a systematic student of anything. How much and what parts
of the Kabbala she actually read, we do not know. But what we
know of her makes it very plausible that she was drawn to some
of the teachings of the Jewish mystics, in whatever way she may
have made their acquaintance.

I propose to have a brief look at a few of these teachings, and
show where they seem to me to correspond to ideas expressed
in her poetry. There is, for instance, the doctrine of reincarnation. About this Gerschon Scholem, in his fundamental book
on Jewish mysticism, has this to say:

> Each individual soul retains its individual existence only until the
> moment when it has worked out its own spiritual restoration . . .
> As long as the soul has not fulfilled this task it remains subject to
> the law of transmigration. Transmigration is thus no longer
> mere retribution, it is also at the same time a chance of fulfilling
> the commandments which it was not given to the soul to fulfil
> before.[1]

We have just mentioned Else Lasker-Schüler's letter to Kraus
in which she described herself as a reincarnation of Joseph:

> In Bagdad sagte mir mal eine Zauberin, ich hätte viele Tausendjahre
> als Mumie im Gewölbe gelegen und sei nicht mehr und nicht
> weniger als Joseph, der auf arabisch Jussuf heißt.   (BK, p. 14)

In *Ich und Ich* she announces 'Vor Sternenjahren weilte ich auf
Erden schon!' (GW, III, 86), and similar ideas can also be found

---

[1] G. Scholem, *Major Trends in Jewish Mysticism*, London, 1955, p. 282.

in her poetry, e.g. when she says of Trakl that 'Er war wohl
Martin Luther' (GW, I, 256), or, when in the poem *Chronica*
she talks about her brothers and sisters:

> Denn drei sind wir Schwestern,
> Die vor mir träumten schon in Sphinxgestalten
> Zu Pharaozeiten; – (. . .)
> Und wisset wer meine Brüder sind?
> Sie waren die drei Könige, die gen Osten zogen
> Dem weißen Sterne nach zum Gotteskind.   (GW, I, 79)

But when, at the end of this somewhat obscure poem, she announces the survival of the evil forces that plagued her family
'über unserem letzten Grabe (. . .) noch', she seems to depart
fundamentally from the mystic teaching according to which
'the last grave' should also bring spiritual restoration, and even
the short extract from Scholem's book shows that Else Lasker-
Schüler's use of the idea of transmigration was comparatively
superficial.

In another sense, however, this doctrine expressed something
with which this poet was deeply acquainted – the 'exile' of the
soul. About this Scholem says:

> The horrors of Exile were mirrored in the Kabbalistic doctrine
> of metempsychosis, which . . . won immense popularity by
> stressing the various stages of the soul's exile. The most terrible
> fate that could befall any soul . . . was to be 'outcast' or 'naked'
> . . . Absolute homelessness was the sinister symbol of absolute
> Godlessness.[1]

In our chapters dealing with Else Lasker-Schüler's 'withdrawal'
we have frequently found this conception of herself as an
exile, an outcast. And we have seen, particularly in the poem
O Ich möcht aus der Welt, to what extent 'homelessness' and
'Godlessness' were associated in her mind, how the eternal
wanderer in her was circling around 'Gottes Grab' (see above,
p. 84).

Another aspect of mystical teaching which we have met in

[1] *Ibid.* p. 250.

Else Lasker-Schüler's work is a tendency towards dualism. The cosmogonic myth that forms the centre of the teachings of one of the most important Kabbalists, Isaac Luria, has distinct affinity with Gnosticism. This myth is summed up by I. Epstein in the following way:

> Central to Luria's system is the doctrine of zimzun (contraction), which conceives creation to have been preceded by a voluntary contraction...of the Infinite...in order to make room for the finite world of phenomena. Into the dark vacuum thus formed the Infinite projected His light, providing it at the same time with the 'vessels' as media for its multifarious manifestations in creation. But some of the 'vessels', unable to endure the inrush of the light . . . broke. The 'breaking of the vessels' caused a deterioration in the worlds above and chaos and confusion in the world below. Instead of its uniform diffusion throughout the universe, the light irradiating from the Infinite was broken up into sparks illumining only certain parts of physical creation while other parts were left in darkness . . . Thus did light and darkness, good and evil, begin to contend for the mastery of the world.[1]

It is now the task of every individual Jew to help to restore the harmony which 'the breaking of the vessels' has destroyed. How is the Jew to accomplish his share in the task of restoration? Let us listen once more to Epstein:

> For the separation of good from evil . . . Luria advocated the practice of asceticism, self-mortification, fastings, and ablutions.[2]

Though Epstein goes on to say that 'Luria still insisted that the body was pure as much as the soul', we can see how small a step there is from this view of redemption of the world through 'self-mortification' to a contempt of the body and a conception of matter as inferior and corrupting – a danger never far away from mystical views of this kind. Else Lasker-Schüler certainly did not always escape it – thus, she speaks in *Ich und Ich* of 'Seelen, die sich noch im Hause leiblicher Gefangenschaft

[1] I. Epstein, *Judaism*, London, 1959, pp. 224-5.
[2] *Ibid.* p. 246.

befinden' (GW, III, 88), and announces in *Konzert*: 'Der Leib ist nur Illusion' (GW, II, 627), to proceed:

> Das ist die Urtragik der Menschenseele, daß sein erdichteter Koloß sie gefährdet . . . Genau wie mein Körper mir im Licht steht, so steht der Weltseele erdichteter Weltkörper ihr im Wege.
>
> *(ibid.* p. 628)

We have already seen her attitude towards sex was troubled by her uneasiness about the body (see above, pp. 103–4), and here perhaps is a point that justifies my preference for speaking of 'affinity' rather than 'influence': for it would, of course, be absurd to suggest that it was the reading of the Kabbalah which made her frequently experience temptation and despair in sexual terms. It is rather that she found her own uneasiness about the role of the 'flesh' expressed in certain dualistic aspects of Jewish mysticism.

This 'dualism' found also expression in her poetry. In looking at *Genesis* we have already come upon the line: 'Und blieb doch Fleisch, leibeigen und verflucht'. The kabbalistic idea of the 'divine sparks' exiled and imprisoned in matter finds a counterpart in these lines in *Gedenktag*:

> Doch meine Seele will von dieser Welt nicht gehen.
> Und hat sich von mir abgewandt.
> Ich wollte immer ihr ein Kleid aus Muscheln nähen;
> In meinen rauhen Körper wurde sie verbannt.   (GW, I, 322)

Her longing for a lost paradise which we have considered in some detail can also be understood in connection with this myth. When she writes:

> Überall hängt noch ein Fetzen Paradies. Gehst du auch daran vorüber – nur einige Menschen erkennen wieder das schimmernd erhaltene Beet allererster Heimat. Die ganze Welt war einmal . . . Paradies (. . .)   (GW, II, 709)

it sounds like a variation on the theme of the exiled 'sparks'. The poem *Im Anfang* (see above, p. 59) is like a naive portrayal of this 'allererste Heimat'. The various poems on the 'Fall' can also be seen in this context (see above, pp. 62–3).

This brings us to the problem of Good and Evil. The Jewish mystic, according to Scholem, answers the old and difficult question about the existence of Evil in a world created by God in a specific way:

> The mystic does not even recoil before the inference that in a higher sense there is a root of evil even in God ... Spheres, which are often described with the aid of mythical metaphors and provide the key for a kind of mystical topography of the Divine realm, are ... nothing but stages in the revelation of God's creative power. Every attribute represents a given stage, including the attribute of severity and stern judgment, which mystical speculation has connected with the source of evil in God.[1]

Epstein, in his account of Luria's cosmogonic myth from which we quoted previously, expressed the kabbalistic approach to this problem in a less paradoxical way:

> ... scattered hither and thither, the sparks of Divine light intersected everywhere the darkness, with the result that evil and good became so mixed that there is no evil that does not contain an element of good, nor is there a good entirely free of evil.[2]

And Else Lasker-Schüler seems to have come across yet another version of this complicated thought:

> (...) wie schon Jesus der Nazarener sagte: 'Die Lauen aber speie ich aus meinem Munde!' Oder wie in unserem heiligen Sohar, dem 1. Buch der Kabbala, steht (nur inhaltlich wiedergegeben): 'Die Zügel des Bösen sollen nicht brüchige, willkürliche Zügel sein'. Gemeint ist damit, daß das Böse gelenkt, nicht Schlechtes anrichtet.   (GW, II, 724-5)

In one of the notes on the poet's letters to Kraus, Gehlhoff-Claes comments on her pre-occupation with this problem:

> Das unbegreifliche Nebeneinander von Gottes Allmacht und Dasein und vom Bösen und Leid in der Welt ist ein Hauptproblem der Gottesauffassung Else Lasker-Schülers und ein Grund ihrer Beschäftigung mit der kabbalistischen Lehre.   (BK, p. 135)

[1] Scholem, *op. cit.* p. 13.
[2] Epstein, *op. cit.* p. 245.

The poem *An Gott* mirrors the poet's concern:

> Du wehrst den guten und den bösen Sternen nicht;
> All ihre Launen strömen.
> In meiner Stirne schmerzt die Furche,
> Die tiefe Krone mit dem düsteren Licht.
>
> Und meine Welt ist still –
> Du wehrtest meiner Laune nicht.
> Gott, wo bist du?
>
> Ich möchte nah an deinem Herzen lauschen,
> Mit deiner fernsten Nähe mich vertauschen,
> Wenn goldverklärt in deinem Reich
> Aus tausendseligem Licht
> Alle die guten und die bösen Brunnen rauschen. (GW, I, 171)

One may be inclined to see in the first two lines of this poem only an expression of the fact that God allows good and evil to exist side by side. But if we remember that the star is a symbol of transcendence, then the existence of 'evil stars' reminds us of the passage (see above, p. 134), in which Scholem says that the Jewish 'mystic does not even recoil before the inference that in a higher sense there is a root of evil even in God'. This interpretation is supported by the last three lines where the stars have become fountains, standing 'goldverklärt' in God's kingdom. In the second part of the first stanza this double aspect of divinity is echoed by the ambiguity of the creative gift: the poet's 'crown' causes pain, its 'light' is 'gloomy'. (The device of the oxymoron appears here as the poetic manifestation of a mystical concept – that of the 'coincidentia oppositorum'.)

In the next stanza God's toleration of good *and* evil is given a personal turn: God allows *her* 'Laune' to exist, and this can here only mean her good *and* evil moods, as the word 'Laune' is used before with reference to the bad *and* evil stars ('All ihre Launen strömen') – and from this a question arises which one might call one of the basic questions of all religion: if God allows both good and evil to exist – who is he then, where is he then? (I am not at all clear about the meaning of 'Und meine Welt ist still' – unless stillness means here that numbness which we met as an aspect of spiritual death – see above, p. 86.)

The last stanza expresses the wish to come closer to an answer to this basic question by coming closer to God, closer to that core of being where the mystery of co-existence of the 'guten und bösen Brunnen' has its origin. God's 'fernste Nähe' is another oxymoron, expressing this time an aspect of the mystical view of divinity. In a letter to Kraus, the poet writes about her experience of God as both close and remote:

> Ich bin ganz gottverlassen oder gerade zwischen seinen Geweiden eingeklemmt. (BK, p. 74)

Gehlhoff-Claes has this note on this sentence:

> Das wechselnde Gefühl der vollkommenen Ferne und der beklemmenden Nähe Gottes ist auch in den Dichtungen immer wieder gestaltet. (*ibid.* p. 135)

And again it is interesting to compare with this Scholem's interpretation of the Jewish mystic's ambivalent approach to God:

> The mystic strives to assure himself of the living presence of God, the God of the Bible, the God who is good, wise, just and merciful . . . But at the same time he is unwilling to renounce the idea of the hidden God who remains unknowable in the depth of His own Self, or, to use the bold expression of the Kabbalists, 'in the depth of His nothingness'.[1]

There are a number of other kabbalistic ideas that attracted Else Lasker-Schüler, but as they did not find any expression in her poetry, only passing reference can be made to them in the context of our enquiry. There is, for instance, the strange concept of God's 'Entdunkelung' which raises once more the question of the role of our body:

> In der Kabbala steht, daß die Gottheit sich entdunkelte, bevor sie die Welt erschuf. Es ist nicht anders zu verstehen, als daß Gott einst einen Körper besaß wie wir, sich selbst erlöste, was wir Sterben nennen, und, ungehemmt der Schale, den Chaos durch-

---

[1] Scholem, *op. cit.* p. 12.

lichtete (. . .) Das heißt: die Gefangenschaft des Körpers verließ und geistig betreut den Weltraum. So bin ich wenigstens nur imstande, den Körper des Menschen zu verstehen, den Gott schuf nach seinem Urebenbilde. Und ich frage mich, warum man dieses Urebenbild verachten soll, das fleischliche, die Hülle der Seele (. . .)   (GW, II, 741–2)

It is interesting how dualistic thoughts ('die Gefangenschaft des Körpers') and others that reject any contempt of the body follow one another.

Another doctrine that fascinated her was Rabbi Luria's description of the creation not as 'an act of revelation but one of limitation' of God where 'God was compelled to make room for the world by, as it were, abandoning a region within Himself'.[1] The strange concept inspired her to the following comment:

Also die Gottheit machte dem Weltall Platz, hinterließ ihm seine Atmosphäre, aus der alles wuchs und gedieh, selbst die Temperaturen, die Eigenschaften der Länder (. . .)   (GW, II, 737)

Lehnt Er sich oder stützt sich an Ihm der von Ihm abgestoßene Raum, den Er Weltall nannte? Wie verhält sich Gott körperlich zur Welt, falls Er sich gestaltete? Rücklings oder seitlich? Anzunehmen angesichtlich.   (*ibid*. p. 738)

These may seem strange speculations, but what is relevant to our examination is the passionate concern with the nature of God and his relation to his creation. There are an infinite number of definitions of mysticism, but if we accept F. C. Happold's description of the mystic as someone who strives 'to break through the world of history and time into that of eternity and timelessness'[2] – and this definition has the virtue of simplicity – then Else Lasker-Schüler's pre-occupation with certain mystical ideas becomes very understandable. For throughout our enquiry we have seen this poet in search of a way either out of 'the world of history and time' which often led her into isolation and despair, or a way through and beyond it which led her to the question: 'Gott, wo bist Du?'

---

[1] *Ibid*. pp. 260–1.   [2] F. C. Happold, *Mysticism*, London, 1963, p. 18.

The Changing Image of God

'Ich habe mich stets befleißigt, nicht nach Gold, aber nach Gott zu graben (. . .)' writes Else Lasker-Schüler in one of her essays which ends with the words: 'Wir können nicht gewaltsam Stufen überspringen, aber wir wollten entdecken, nach Gott graben, bis wir auf Ihn stoßen' (GW, II, 740 and 743). Her search for God – she uses the more concrete expression 'digging' which gives a feeling of the effort, even the pain involved – was certainly a matter of 'steps', a life-long development whereby the image of what she was searching for was continuously changing. For once, it is appropriate to speak of 'development' – for though the various 'images' of God occur frequently side by side, there is a definite movement from the 'Verkindlichung' of God in, say, *Im Anfang* (see above, pp. 59–60) to the acceptance of God as creator and person, the 'Thou' of Buber's interpretation.

The image of God that we met in *Im Anfang* appears also in the poem *O Gott*:

> Überall nur kurzer Schlaf
> Im Mensch, im Grün, im Kelch der Winde.
> Jeder kehrt in sein totes Herz beim.
>
> – Ich wollt die Welt wär noch ein Kind –
> Und wüßte mir vom ersten Atem zu erzählen.
>
> Früher war eine große Frömmigkeit am Himmel,
> Gaben sich die Sterne die Bibel zu lesen.
> Könnte ich einmal Gottes Hand fassen
> Oder den Mond an seinem Finger sehn.
>
> O Gott, o Gott, wie weit bin ich von dir!   (GW, I, 214)

The first stanza introduces an idea which we already met in *An meine Freunde* (see above, p. 99). 'Schlaf' is, once more, not the 'tote Ruhe', the dead numbness which is an aspect of despair – it is a life-giving state, common to man and nature, and here only of brief duration: waking up from it means a return into one's 'dead heart'.

The next step from such a state of spiritual death is, as before, one of withdrawal – the withdrawal into the fantasy of a childhood paradise. The first line of the second stanza echoes the second line of *Im Anfang* ('Als die Welt noch Kind war') – the poet wishes that the world were still young, a 'Spielgefährte' (GW, I, 315) who would tell her how it was 'in the beginning'. The third stanza gives an idyllic description of this childhood paradise where all was still well. God appears again as someone whom one could call, as in *Im Anfang*, 'junger Vater', as a benevolent, protective, personified (as against 'personal') God. The last line, however, is a simple naked expression of God's distance, and thus already on a different plane from the whimsical 'Ja, ja, / Als ich noch Gottes Schlingel war' with which *Im Anfang* ends.

Und suche Gott presents a very different image of God:

> Ich habe immer vor dem Rauschen meines Herzens gelegen,
> Nie den Morgen gesehen,
> Nie Gott gesucht.
> Nun aber wandle ich um meines Kindes
> Goldgedichtete Glieder
> Und suche Gott.
>
> Ich bin müde vom Schlummer,
> Weiß nur vom Antlitz der Nacht.
> Ich fürchte mich vor der Frühe,
> Sie hat ein Gesicht
> Wie die Menschen, die fragen.
>
> Ich habe immer vor dem Rauschen meines Herzens gelegen;
> Nun aber taste ich um meines Kindes
> Gottgelichtete Glieder. (GW, I, 167)

In this poem, Else Lasker-Schüler sees in her love for her son Paul a turning-point in her approach to God: it is in the child that her search begins. She describes this in the first stanza. The first line of the poem is not easy to interpret – 'Ich habe immer vor dem Rauschen meines Herzens gelegen' could mean 'I have always obstructed the sound of my heart – so that it could not reach its true aim, God.' Such a meaning is also suggested by the following two lines. The morning is here a symbol for the beginning, the source of things, and thus for God the creator. The remaining three lines of the stanza present the turning-point:

now that there is another being in her world, a child whose limbs seem miraculously 'goldgedichtet', the question of the 'Dichter', the creator, arises.

The second stanza elaborates the ideas of the first three lines. It takes up her lament that she has 'never seen the morning': she describes herself as night-bound, unrefreshed by sleep (which is here once more 'die tote Ruhe'), lost in darkness and confusion, afraid to meet the ordering, sense-giving questions of the morning. Among these questions there is also the question of God.

The third stanza, in turn, varies the second part of the first. (There is a greater degree of structural organization in her work than appears at first sight.) Instead of

> Nun aber *wandle* ich um meines Kindes
> *goldgedichtete* Glieder

we have now

> Nun aber *taste* ich um meines Kindes
> *gottgelichtete* Glieder.

'Tasten' is more concrete than 'wandeln' – it gives physical expression to her 'groping'. The change from 'goldgedichtet' to 'gottgelichtet', 'illuminated by God', expresses a kind of incarnation of the Divine in the body of her child. A repetition of the title line 'Und suche Gott' is not necessary – 'tasten' and 'gottgelichtet' imply this idea in a more substantial form.

We remember at this point that it was the death of this deeply beloved son that, far from leading to a rejection of God, made her see more clearly that the 'image' of God was indeed love:

> Die Liebe zu dir ist das Bildnis,
> Das man sich von Gott machen darf.

(See above, pp. 91–2)

But God, in these poems, is still remote, is not yet someone to whom one can speak, whom one can expect to listen. Such a God we meet in *Gott hör . . .*:

> Um meine Augen zieht die Nacht sich
> Wie ein Ring zusammen.
> Mein Puls verwandelte das Blut in Flammen
> Und doch war alles grau und kalt um mich.

O Gott und bei lebendigem Tage,
Träum ich vom Tod.
Im Wasser trink ich ihn und würge ihn im Brot.
Für meine Traurigkeit gibt es kein Maß auf deiner Waage.

Gott hör . . . In deiner blauen Lieblingsfarbe
Sang ich das Lied von deines Himmels Dach –
Und weckte doch in deinem ewigen Hauche nicht den Tag.
Mein Herz schämt sich vor dir fast seiner tauben Narbe.

Wo ende ich? – O Gott!! Denn in die Sterne,
Auch in den Mond sah ich, in alle deiner Früchte Tal.
Der rote Wein wird schon in seiner Beere schal . . .
Und überall – die Bitternis – in jedem Kerne.   (GW, I, 321)

The first stanza sets the mood: night, once again a dark and
sterile power, restricts her vision, her blood is aflame but cannot
break through the shell of grey coldness that surrounds her.
The first three lines of the following stanza conjure up that
experience of death-in-life which we have met as a frequently
recurring expression of her furthest withdrawal (see above, pp.
85–90). Water and bread are no longer life-givers, but carriers of
death. The fourth line voices her doubt that God, now already
experienced in a very personal way, could measure the full weight
of her sadness.

The beginning of the next stanza repeats the appeal of the
title. This stanza is not easy to interpret. In the first two lines,
she refers to her vocation as a poet: she has sung about God's
dwelling, using his 'favourite colour' blue (see above, p. 49).
But, the next line seems to say, God did not respond, his 'eternal
breath' spelt no hope ('Tag') for her. The fourth line could
perhaps be understood like this: her heart has been wounded
(by someone's hurt? by her own despair? by God's lack of
response?), but the wound is no longer alive, it is a scar and
sterile ('taub'). She is ashamed that her suffering has not borne
any fruit.

'Wo ende ich?', at the beginning of the last stanza, can have
three meanings: where are my limits? how will I die? where will
my despair get me to? The following lines make the third meaning

appear likely (though there is probably something of all three implied): she found bitterness in everything: neither heaven (stars, moon) nor earth (fruit, vine) offer any answer to her despair.

The poem ends on a note of hopelessness: God does not seem to listen. All the same, it marks an important stage in the poet's search: for she is here in a dialogue with God, he is no longer the finger-wagging daddy of *Im Anfang*, nor the only dimly recognized, remote creator of *Und suche Gott*, but already someone to cry out to, even though he does not seem to answer.

We have met this 'personal' image of God in other poems like *Ein Lied an Gott* ('Wie soll ich dich erkennen lieber Gott') and *Letzter Abend im Jahr* ('O Gott, wie kann der Mensch verstehen / Warum der Mensch haltlos vom Menschtum bricht'). In these poems (see above, pp. 55 and 71–2), the relation with God has become 'personal', in the sense of being one from person to person, the kind of relationship to the Divine that William Barrett calls specifically Hebrew, and which he sees exemplified in the relation between Job and God:

> The Hebrew . . . proceeds not by the way of reason but by the confrontation of the whole man, Job, in the fulness and violence of his passion with the unknowable and overwhelming God. And the final solution for Job lies not in the rational resolution of the problem . . . but in a change and conversion of the whole man.[1]

The Bible is, of course, essentially the record of this relationship between God and man, and Else Lasker-Schüler, in some of her *Hebräische Balladen*, expressed this in her own way – as, for instance, in the statement that Abraham 'übte sich mit Gott zu reden' (GW, I, 294), or when she expressed Jacob's closeness to God by saying that their beards resembled each other:

> So oft sprach Jakob inbrünstig zu seinem Herrn,
> Sie trugen gleiche Bärte, Schaum, von einer Eselin gemolken.
>
> (GW, I, 298)

[1] W. Barrett, *Irrational Man*, London, 1961, p. 65.

But in poems like *Gott hör* . . . and *Ein Lied an Gott*, God though experienced as someone to be questioned remains remote, inscrutable, a God to be rebelled against rather than to be trusted. Yet another step had to be made, yet another 'Stufe' to be overcome before inner peace was reached. This happened increasingly in the poems of her last years, e.g. in *Gebet*:

> Oh Gott, ich bin voll Traurigkeit . . .
> Nimm mein Herz in deine Hände –
> Bis der Abend geht zu Ende
> In steter Wiederkehr der Zeit.
>
> Oh Gott, ich bin so müd, oh, Gott,
> Der Wolkenmann und seine Frau
> Sie spielen mit mir himmelblau
> Im Sommer immer, lieber Gott.
>
> Und glaube unserm Monde, Gott,
> Denn er umhüllte mich mit Schein,
> Als wär ich hilflos noch und klein,
> – Ein Flämmchen Seele.
>
> Oh, Gott und ist sie auch voll Fehle –
> Nimm sie still in deine Hände . . .
> Damit sie leuchtend in dir ende.   (GW, I, 338)

Here we find once more some of the themes previously discussed. Again, in the first stanza, she turns to God out of a dark mood. But it is sadness here, not despair! Again, evening is feared and morning awaited. But there is a new simplicity, a humility which expresses itself in a line like, 'Nimm mein Herz in deine Hände'. We are reminded of Paul Gerhardt and Mathias Claudius.

In the second stanza, the theme of childhood play returns, a reference to a past idyllic state for which she longs in her present tiredness. This state is still for her identical with the idea of spiritual peace – the game which the cloud-man and his wife play with her is 'sky-blue'.

Of this there is also something in the following stanza where she calls the moon as witness for her childlike helplessness – did he not protect her with his cloak of light, 'a little flame of a soul'?

But though the element of withdrawal into a childhood world is familiar, the tone is new: there is nothing of the forced jollity, the sometimes embarrassing prettification we find in some of her earlier poems. The note that prevails here is one of recognition of her limitations.

This is emphasized by the last stanza: if God takes her soul into his hands, with all its imperfections, it will come to a radiant 'end'. Despair has given way to acceptance. The creature is ready to rest in the hands of the Creator.

There are a number of poetic fragments published by Werner Kraft as part of Else Lasker-Schüler's *Nachlaß* which breathe a similar spirit. For instance, this:

> O Gott, ich bin so müde.
> Von Augenlid zu Augenlide
> Schwimmt mein Gedanke hin.
> Und bin nicht wo ich bin,
> Das Lied in der Etüde,
> Das stille Blau im Sinn –
> Nimm von mir all Gewinn
> Und kommt einmal der Friede . . .   (GW, III, 115)

The Figure of Christ

We have still to consider one other aspect of Else Lasker-Schüler's approach to God – her relation to the figure of Christ. This would in itself warrant an intensive study which, however, would go beyond the context of our theme. For she did not write any poems about Christ, and it is her poetry with which we are concerned here. There are, however, a number of indirect references to Christ in her poetry, and she has shown her passionate interest in him in her prose writings. I feel that no examination of her religious development can ignore her deep involvement with the 'Messias, der schon einmal auf Erden wandelte' (GW, II, 750), an event for which, as she said 'weder die Juden noch alle anderen Völker reif waren es zu bewerten und zu bewahren in seiner Echtheit' (*ibid.*).

For someone so deeply conscious of her Jewishness, this

belief in Christ could not have been easy to sustain and was bound to fluctuate. Thus she writes in one of her letters to Walden which came to form part of her 'Briefroman' *Mein Herz*:

> ..., ich habe kein Interesse für das Wohlergehen dieser Welt mehr, schwärme nur noch für ihren ärmsten Tand; Schaumglaskugeln in allen sanften Farben, manche sind wie kleine Altäre geformt, in ihrer Nische leuchten verborgene Schimmerblumen der Maria. Ich glaube schon, ich spüre die gläsernen Blüten in der Brust. Diese Offenbarung! Und bin doch keine Christin; wo könnte ich an mir Christin werden? Das hieße sein Blut verstoßen. Diese Erkenntnis sollte des Jehovavolkes hochmütigster Reichtum sein. (GW, II, 355)

And while she could write about the incarnation as any faithful Christian:

> Er sandte (. . .) seinen Sohn, das heißt, er kam in Menschgestalt zur Erde. Solcher Umgestaltung Demut vom Stern zum Chaos ist nur ein Gott fähig (GW, II, 150)

– Radetzky's memoir shows a more doubting approach:

> Sie klagte, daß 'die Christen' die Gestalt Jesu verfälscht und versüßlicht hätten. Mehrmals geschah es, daß sie plötzlich innehielt und mit großen Augen sagte: 'Wie, wenn Er wirklich Gottes Sohn gewesen wäre . . . (DD, p. 581)

I say 'doubting' – but perhaps it would be more correct to speak of longing. For someone who had experienced God as remote and unscrutable, withdrawn from his creation, silent to his creature's urgent pleas, the possibility of 'solcher Umgestaltung Demut', of the incarnation, must have appeared as the answer to all her questions.

The fact that she never made Christ directly the theme of her poems testifies perhaps to the difficulties she must have felt with this belief in a figure whom the Jews either regarded as another prophet, or altogether rejected. The closest she comes to actually mentioning Christ is at the beginning of *Der gefallene Engel* (see above, p. 62) with a line that, in its comparison of Peter Hille with the 'Nazarener', announces her conception of the poet-vagabond as a kind of 'saviour'.

In two other instances she conceived people who were very close to her as 'saviours': in a poem dedicated to her brother Paul which starts

> Der Du bist auf Erden gekommen,
> Mich zu erlösen
> Aus aller Pein (. . .)   (GW, I, 47)

and again when, in a prose poem, she lets Franz Marc say, in a variation of one of the sayings of Christ:

> (. . .) und was du namentlich an den Pferden, da sie unbeschreiblich auf dem Schlachtfeld leiden müssen, Gutes tust, tust du mir.   (GW, I, 270)

In the lines already quoted from *Chronica* (see above, p. 131)

> Und wisset wer meine Brüder sind?
> Sie waren die drei Könige, die gen Osten zogen
> Dem weißen Sterne nach zum Gotteskind (. . .)

the 'Gotteskind' seems to symbolize a reconciling power, the aim of her brothers', and her own, search. Christmas was for her truly the feast of reconciling love; *Weihnachten* (GW, I, 324) is a love poem with a Christmas setting, and the prose piece of the same title in *Nachlaß* ends with a poem in which the lovers' extinct feelings are symbolized by Christmas trees after the feast:

> Wir welken längst wo angelehnt,
> Am grauen Steine einer alten Mauer;
> So ausgelöscht (. . .)   (GW, III, 69)

We meet the 'Gotteskind' once more in *Marie von Nazareth* – as 'Gottlingchen' in a folksong-like poem that is almost a nursery rhyme:

> Alle Kinder kommen auf Lämmern
> Zottehotte geritten,
> Gottlingchen sehen –   (GW, I, 172)

Mary makes yet another appearance in Else Lasker-Schüler's poetry, in *Der Mensch* which begins with the lines:

> In deinem Blick schweben
> Alle Himmel zusammen.
>
> Immer hast du die Madonna angesehn,
> Darum sind deine Augen überirdisch.   (GW, I, 242)

The full impact of the figure of Mary she expressed, however, once more not in a poem, but in prose:

> Denken Sie an Maria, durch die Gott schritt (. . .) Sie leidet
> das höchste Fest durch das Gottwillkommen, sieben Schwerter
> krankt ihr Herz. (GW, II, 146)

Perhaps more important even than these references are distinctly Christian undertones in some of her poems. I have already drawn attention to the Christian feeling of the lines

> Die heilige Liebe, die ihr blind zertratet,
> Ist Gottes Ebenbild . . .!
> Fahrlässig umgebracht (. . .)

which sounds like a paraphrase of the crucifixion (see above, pp. 48–50). We have also seen an approximation to Christian values in the 'correction' of the Old Testament commandment in these lines on the death of her son:

> Die Liebe zu dir ist das Bildnis
> Das man sich von Gott machen darf.
> (See above, pp. 91–2)

To this I would like to add the second stanza of *Herbst*:

> Das ewige Leben *dem*, der viel von Liebe weiß zu sagen.
> Ein Mensch der *Liebe* kann nur auferstehen!
> Haß schachtelt ein! wie hoch die Fackel auch mag schlagen.
> (GW, I, 351)

Here the idea of resurrection, never central to Jewish doctrine, is linked with a specifically Christian concept of love -- a love that is no longer a demand for being loved.

Else Lasker-Schüler's devotion to the figure of Christ, her acceptance of certain Christian ideas while at the same time stressing her Jewishness and refusing to become a Christian – all this may strike many people as strange and contradictory, and has probably increased the antagonism which was never very far away wherever she went. But she could not accept the division of religion into various denominations. Thus, Catherine Küster-Ginsberg heard her say:

> Meint ihr wirklich, daß Gott die Religionen gewollt hat?
> Jüdisch, Katholisch, Protestantisch, ich glaub's nicht. Ist denn
> ein Tiger katholisch?[1]

And in the last scene of her autobiographical play *Arthur Aronymus und seine Väter*, a Bishop is invited to the Jewish Easter celebration, and after one of the main characters, modelled on her great-grandmother, has said:

> Und mit einem bißchen Liebe gehts schon, daß Jude und Christ
> ihr Brot *gemeinsam in Eintracht brechen*, noch wenn es ungesäuert
> gereicht wird (. . .)   (GW, II, 1193)

the Bishop ends the play with these words:

> Meine geliebten Brüder und Schwestern in Christo! Von tiefer
> Freude ist mein Herz bewegt. In dieser Stunde, in der ich als
> Mittler stehe zwischen euch *vor* diesem Hause und denen *in*
> diesem Hause, erfüllt sich mir das Wort unseres heiligen Apostels
> Petrus, der da sagte: 'Gott sieht nicht auf die Person, vielmehr
> ist ihm in jedem Volke wohlgefällig, wer ihn fürchtet und recht
> tut.'   (*ibid.*)

Else Lasker-Schüler's deep need for communication which, as we have seen, is at the very root of her being, expressed itself nowhere more clearly, more passionately, than in this wish for reconciliation. It is as 'reconciliation', I think, rather than as 'atonement', that she understood the meaning of the greatest Jewish feast, the 'Versöhnungstag' which she described in one of her most beautiful essays (GW, II, 743ff.) and to which the following poem refers – a poem that draws together a number of the themes close to her heart:

> *Versöhnung*
>
> Es wird ein großer Stern in meinen Schoß fallen . . .
> Wir wollen wachen die Nacht,
>
> In den Sprachen beten,
> Die wie Harfen eingeschnitten sind.

---

[1] Küster, *op. cit.*

Wir wollen uns versöhnen die Nacht –
So viel Gott strömt über.

Kinder sind unsere Herzen,
Die möchten ruhen müdesüß.

Und unsere Lippen wollen sich küssen,
Was zagst du?

Grenzt nicht mein Herz an deins –
Immer färbt dein Blut meine Wangen rot.

Wir wollen uns versöhnen die Nacht,
Wenn wir uns herzen, sterben wir nicht.

Es wird ein großer Stern in meinen Schoß fallen.

(GW, I, 155)

The first line of this poem already brings an image of reconciliation: spirit and flesh become one, the symbol of transcendence, the star, is – in the widest sense – received into the 'womb' of earthly creativeness. The next five lines refer more directly to the feast – to the vigil (Jewish feasts always start in the evening), the prayers (with the beautiful harp-metaphor for the Hebrew letters), the act of mutual 'Versöhnung' which is only possible because of God's abundant presence.

The next stanza introduces the familiar theme of childhood as a state of rest and peacefulness. The following three stanzas have a more personal note: the love between two human beings becomes part of that greater union of which the third stanza speaks. 'Wenn wir uns herzen, sterben wir nicht', using the word 'herzen' in its original strong meaning, announces with great simplicity another theme we have met before: where there is true communion, there is no death. Finally, the beginning is repeated, the essence of 'Versöhnung' as the transcendence of all division restated.

Jerusalem

Else Lasker-Schüler hoped to find 'Versöhnung' concretized in Jerusalem. This capital of the Holy Land, holy to both Jew and Christian, had haunted her imagination since she was a child.

'Ich habe als Kind so oft Jerusalem gezeichnet', she writes (GW, II, 907). And again, in *Reliquie*:

> Ich sah nie unsere heilige Stadt im Herrn,
> Sie rief mich oft im Traum des Windes.　　(GW, I, 319)

But when she actually came to the 'heilige Stadt im Herrn', she was disappointed. Once more, the discrepancy between image and reality was too great. She wrote from Jerusalem:

> Nach schweren Tagen: Grüße! Es ist zu schwer für mich unterm Volke hier. David wäre – auch abgereist.　　(DD, p. 560)

> Nicht zu schildern an Verwunderung und Handel und Meer und Dunkelheit. Hier: *herrliches* Bibelland, Karawanen fortwährend am Balkon vorbei. Ganz anders wie man sich vorstellt. Aber *schwer*.　　(*ibid.* p. 533)

Her poem *Jerusalem* starts with the lines

> Ich wandele wie durch Mausoleen –
> Versteint ist unsere Heilige Stadt (. . .)　　(GW, I, 334)

and later in the poem a line expresses her feeling about what she felt to be the city's spiritual deadness: 'Jerusalem – erfahre Auferstehen!' One important aspect of her disillusionment was the lack of recognition by her people. C. Küster-Ginsberg writes:

> Als Armutsbündel reiste diese jüdische Dichterin in die von ihr besungene und ersehnte Heimat. Dort erwartete sie ein Hungerleben. Alt, gebrechlich, kurios wirkend, war sie eine Fremde.[1]

Nevertheless, the hope that Jerusalem would bring one nearer to 'Versöhnung' because of the greater presence of God did not leave her:

> 'Ist Gott? Ja, ist er denn nun wirklich?' so begann sie zu fragen, wenn ihr unruhiges Herz es verlangte. 'In Jerusalem ist man ihm manchmal näher, nein?'[2]

[1] Küster, *op. cit.*
[2] *Ibid.*

But the Jerusalem she really meant was somewhere else. Many years before she went to Palestine she had reported a dream in one of her essays:

> Einmal hatte Jesus Christus in der Nacht im Mond gesessen, ich schlief zwar, aber er kam im Traum zu mir ganz nahe an mein Bett und sagte: 'Jerusalem ist nicht verloren, da es in deinem Herzen wohnt.'
>
> (GW, II, 715)

It was this Jerusalem that 'lived in her heart' that makes its sudden appearance in *Ich schlafe in der Nacht* at the point where the lovers' union is complete:

> (. . .) unsere Seelen schweben übers Heilige Land
> In *einem* Sternenkleide leuchtend um die Lenden.
>
> (See above, pp. 63–4)

That she was deeply aware that *her* Jerusalem could not be confined to one particular place in one particular country she shows in a passage in her book about Palestine, *Das Hebräerland*:

> Der alte Friedhof, auf dem meine Eltern schlummern und mein frommer, aschblonder Bruder, ein Heiliger (. . .) ist Erde von Jerusalemerde, vom Erdfleisch des Gelobten Bodens. Jerusalem ist überall zwischen uns Menschen im Leben und im Tod. Jerusalem reicht uns die Hand, geleitet uns zu beiden Wegen. Jerusalem heißt unser Engel in jedem Lande, in jedem Erdteil – sehnen wir ihn nur herbei.
>
> (GW, II, 876–7)

Conclusion

We have reached the point where our pendulum comes to rest. We have traced its movement backwards from disappointment through despair to flight into fantasy and the wish for death. We have traced its movement forwards from a longing for friendship through the hazards of the erotic encounter to a search for the Thou behind all thous, God. In whatever direction the movement went, we always found as its driving impulse a deep longing for contact, a passionate concern with communication. We have also seen that it was increasingly in her search for God, in her groping towards the acceptance of an extra-human reality, that

Else Lasker-Schüler came closest to 'Versöhnung', a reconciliation, a lifting of the opposing forces in herself on to another plane
where the 'break' in her world came closer to healing.

On this plane, our image of the pendulum that swings in either
one direction or the other can no longer serve as a model. It is
a plane where perhaps all metaphors must become silent, and the
most complex experience has to find its most simple expression,
as it does in the poem where Else Lasker-Schüler commends her
soul to God:

> Oh Gott, und ist sie auch voll Fehle –
> Nimm sie still in deine Hände . . .
> Damit sie leuchtend in dir ende.

BIOGRAPHICAL DATA

Life		Work	
1869	Birth in Wuppertal-Elberfeld.		
1890	Death of mother.		
1894	Marries Dr Lasker; goes to Berlin.		
1897	Death of father.		
1899	Marriage breaks down; meets Alcibiades de Rouan.	1899	First poems published in *Die Gesellschaft*.
1900	Birth of son Paul.		
1901	Marries Georg Levin (Herwarth Walden).		
		1902	*Styx, Gedichte*, Berlin.
1904	Walden founds 'Verein für die Kunst'. Death of Peter Hille.		
		1905	*Der siebente Tag, Gedichte*, Berlin.
		1906	*Das Peter Hille-Buch*, Stuttgart and Berlin.
		1907	*Die Nächte der Tino von Bagdad*, Berlin, Stuttgart and Leipzig.
		1909	*Die Wupper, Schauspiel*, Berlin.
1910	*Der Sturm*.		
1911	Divorce from Walden; meets Franz Marc.	1911	*Meine Wunder, Gedichte*, Leipzig.
		1911–12	'Briefe nach Norwegen', in: *Der Sturm*.
1912	Meets Gottfried Benn.	1912	*Mein Herz, Ein Liebesroman*, Munich and Berlin.
1913	Collection to relieve her poverty, announced in *Die Fackel*.	1913	*Gesichte, Essays*, Leipzig. *Hebräische Balladen*, Berlin.
1914	Meets Georg Trakl.	1913–14	'Briefe und Bilder', in: *Die Aktion*.
		1914	'Der Malik, Briefe an den blauen Reiter Franz Marc', in: *Der Brenner*.

Life		*Work*	
			Der Prinz von Theben, Ein Geschichtenbuch, Leipzig.
			'Plumm-Pascha', in: *Das Kinobuch,* Leipzig.
		1915	'Briefe an den blauen Reiter', in: *Die Aktion.*
		1917	'Der Malik', in: *Neue Jugend.*
			Die gesammelten Gedichte, Leipzig.
1919	First performance of *Die Wupper* in Berlin.	1919	*Der Malik, Eine Kaisergeschichte,* Berlin.
		1920	*Hebräische Balladen, Der Gedichte erster Teil,* Berlin.
			Die Kuppel, Der Gedichte zweiter Teil, Berlin.
			Gesichte, 2. Aufl. (with two new pieces), Berlin.
			Essays (= *Gesichte* with some new pieces), Berlin.
			Die gesammelten Gedichte, Munich.
		1921	*Der Wunderrabbiner von Barcelona, Erzählung,* Berlin.
1925	Another collection organized by friends.	1925	*Ich räume auf! Meine Anklage gegen meine Verleger,* Zurich.
1927	Death of Paul.	(c. 1927)	*Die Wupper,* Neuaufl., Selbstverlag.
1932	Kleist-Preis.	1932	*Konzert,* Berlin.
			Arthur Aronymus, Die Geschichte meines Vaters, Berlin.
			Arthur Aronymus und seine Väter; Schauspiel, Berlin.
			Joseph und seine Brüder; Schauspiel (lost).
1933	Emigration to Switzerland.		
1934	Journey to Alexandria and Palestine; return to Switzerland.		

Life		*Work*	
1936	First performance of *Arthur Aronymus* in Zurich.		
1937	Second journey to Palestine; return to Switzerland.	1937	*Das Hebräerland*, Zurich.
1940–1	Final journey to Palestine, settling down in Jerusalem.		
		(c. 1943)	*Ich und Ich, Schauspiel. Mein blaues Klavier, Neue Gedichte*, Jerusalem.
1945	22 January: Death.		

SELECT BIBLIOGRAPHY

I. *Works and Letters*, published posthumously (works published during the poet's lifetime are mentioned under 'Biographical Data').

Else Lasker-Schüler. *Eine Einführung in ihr Werk und eine Auswahl*, hrag. v. W. Kraft (Verschollene und Vergessene), Wiesbaden, 1951.

Dichtungen und Dokumente, ausgew. u. hrsg. u. E. Ginsberg, Munich, 1951.

Gesammelte Werke in drei Bänden, hrsg. v. F. Kemp und W. Kraft, Munich, 1959–61.

Briefe an Karl Kraus, hrsg. v. A. Gehlhoff-Claes, Cologne/Berlin, 1959.

Helles Schlafen – dunkles Wachen, hrsg. v. F. Kemp, Munich, 1962.

Die Wupper/Arthur Aronymus und seine Väter, Munich, 1965.

Sämtliche Gedichte, hrsg. v. F. Kemp, Munich, 1966.

II. *Books, dissertations and articles on the poet and her work*

Aker, E. *Untersuchungen der Lyrik Else Lasker-Schülers*, Diss., Munich, 1956.

Bauschinger, S. *Die Symbolik des Mütterlichen im Werke Else Lasker-Schülers*, Diss., Frankfurt-Main, 1960.

Ben-Chorin, Sch. 'Prinz Jussuf in Jerusalem', *Tribüne*, I, No. 3, Frankfurt, 1962.

Benn, G. 'Else Lasker-Schüler', *Gesammelte Werke*, II, Wiesbaden, 1959.

Fischer, M. 'Else Lasker-Schüler', *Das literarische Echo*, Berlin, 1918–19.

Ginsberg, E. 'Es steigen aus verstaubten Himmelstruhen', *Frankfurter Allgemeine Zeitung*, No. 13, 1965.

Goldstein, F. *Der expressionistische Stilwille im Werke der Else Lasker-Schüler*, Diss., Vienna, 1936.

Guder, G. *Else Lasker-Schüler, Deutung ihrer Lyrik*, Siegen, 1966.

Herzfelde, W. 'Fremd und Nah. Über meinen Briefwechsel und meine Begegnungen mit Else Lasker-Schüler', *Marginalien, Blätter der Pirckheimer-Gesellschaft*, No. 18, Berlin/Weimar, 1965.

Heselhaus, C. 'Else Lasker-Schülers literarisches Traumspiel', in his *Deutsche Lyrik der Moderne*, Düsseldorf, 1961.

Hilty, H. R. 'Ein nachgelassenes Drama der Else Lasker-Schüler', in his *Jeanne d'Arc bei Schiller und Anouilh, Skizzen zu einer Geistesgeschichte des modernen Dramas*, St. Gallen, 1960.

Höltgen, K. J. *Untersuchungen zur Lyrik Else Lasker-Schülers*, Diss., Bonn, 1955 (veränderte Druckfassung: Bonn, 1958).

Kesting, M. 'Zur Dichtung Else Lasker-Schülers', *Akzente*, No. 3, Munich, 1956.

'Else Lasker-Schüler und ihr blaues Klavier', *Deutsche Rundschau*, No. 83, Baden-Baden, 1957.

Kraft, W. 'Erinnerungen an Else Lasker-Schüler', *Hochland*, XLIII, No. 6, Munich, 1951.

'Im Gedenken Else Lasker-Schülers', *Neue Züricher Zeitung*, 30. 1. 1955. (Reprinted as 'Die Dichterin' in *Jahresring* 58–59, Stuttgart, 1958.)

'Else Lasker-Schüler', in his *Wort und Gedanke*, Kritischen Bemerkungen zur Poesie, Bern/Munich, 1959.

'Die Muschel', *Wort und Gedanke*.

Kraus, K. Anmerkung zum 'Tibetteppich', *Die Fackel*, XII, Nos. 313–14, Vienna, 1910.

Kupper, M. *Die Weltanschauung Else Lasker-Schülers in ihren poetischen Selbstzeugnissen*, Diss., Würzburg, 1963.

'Materialien zu einer kritischen Ausgabe der Lyrik Else Lasker-Schülers' (Diss. part II), *Jahrbuch der Görres-Gesellschaft*, New Series, IV, 1963.

'Ein wiederentdecktes Gedicht von Else Lasker-Schüler', *Germanisch-Romanische Monatsschrift*, New Series, XIII, Heidelberg, 1963.

Küster, K. 'Else Lasker-Schüler zum Gedächtnis', *Blick in die Welt*, No. 18, Hamburg, 1947.

Marc, M. *Franz Marc, Botschaften an den Prinzen Jussuf*, Munich, 1954.

Martini, F. *Was war Expressionismus?*, Urach, 1948.

Meyer, F. A. *Ver"weh"te Klänge aus dem Werke der Lasker-Schüler*, Jerusalem, 1946 (unpub. MS).

Muschg, W. 'Else Lasker-Schüler', in his *Von Trakl zu Brecht, Dichter des Expressionismus*, Munich, 1961.

Pankok, H. 'Else Lasker-Schüler', *Die Volksbühne*, V, Düsseldorf, 1952.

Politzer, H. 'The Blue Piano of Else Lasker-Schüler', *Commentary* IX, New York, 1950.

Rychner, M. *Arachne*, Aurich, 1957.

Schlocker, G. 'Else Lasker-Schüler', in *Expressionismus*, ed. H. Friedman and O. Mann, Heidelberg, 1956.

Springmann, W. (ed.) *Else Lasker-Schüler und Wuppertal*, Wuppertal-Elberfeld, 1962.

Sturmann, M. 'Briefe an Else Lasker-Schüler, Zur Einführung', *Bull. for Sponsoring and Contributing Members of the Leo Baeck Institute*, Tel Aviv, 1959.

Wallmann, J. P. *Else Lasker-Schüler*, Mühlacker, 1966.

Weiß, R. 'Else Lasker-Schüler', *Die Fackel*, XIII, Nos. 321–22, Vienna, 1911.

Zweig, A. 'Else Lasker-Schüler 50 Jahre', *Jüdische Rundschau*, XXXI, Berlin, 1926.

SELECT BIBLIOGRAPHY

III. *Some important books published after completion of this study*

Bänsch, D. *Else Lasker-Schüler, Zur Kritik eines etablierten Bildes*, Stuttgart, 1972.

Kupper, M. (ed.) *Lieber gestreifter Tiger, Briefe von Else Lasker-Schüler*, Band I, Munich, 1969.

Wo ist unser buntes Theben, Briefe von Else Lasker-Schüler, Band II, Munich, 1969.

Schmid, M. (ed.) *Else Lasker-Schüler: ein Buch zum 100. Geburtstag der Dichterin*, Wuppertal, 1969.

INDEX

archetypes, theory of, 7–8

Barrett, William, 142
Bauschinger, Sigrid, 2, 7–8, 11, 64, 65, 66
Beardsley, M. C., 3
Ben-Chorin, Schalom, 17
Benn, Gottfried, 9, 26, 27–9, 36, 41, 70, 76, 77, 79
Bible, 31, 58, 79, 80, 122–9, 142
Bollnow, O. F., 54
Brentano, Bettina, 8
Buber, Martin, 117, 118, 138
Burke, Kenneth, 4

Christian references, 94, 144–9
Claudius, Mathias, 143
collections and cycles of poems:
 An Ihn, 47
 Der Siebente Tag, 24
 Gottfried Benn, 70
 Hebräische Balladen, 31, 58, 78–80, 123–4, 142
 Mein blaues Klavier, 100
 Meine Wunder, 10, 26, 39
 Styx, 1, 24
criticism:
 and biography, 1–6, 8
 continuum criticism, 4
 the New Criticism, 2, 3, 5

Däubler, Theodor, 98
Dehmel, Richard, 31, 50
dualism, 132–3

Ehrenbaum-Degele, Hans, 87
Eliot, T. S., 2, 58
Epstein, I., 132, 134
erotic anarchism, 24
essays:
 Das heilige Abendmahl, 100
 Der Prinz von Theben (collection), 31, 79
 Freundschaft und Liebe, 95–6, 97, 102
 Gesichte (collection), 31
 Ich räume auf, 53, 85
 Konzert (collection), 33, 100, 133
 Meine Andacht, 122
 Paradiese, 104

existentialism, 54
expressionism, 8, 9, 15, 23, 25–6

Ficker, Ludwig von, 51
Fischer, Max, 108
Freud, S., 8, 81, 82
Friedrich, Hugo, 123
friendship, 95–102

Gehloff-Claes, Astrid, 15, 16, 17, 18, 20, 23, 24, 27, 28, 29, 88, 129–30, 134, 136
Gerhardt, Paul, 143
Ginsberg, Catherine, *see* Küster-Ginsberg
Goldstein, Fanni, 9
Graves, Robert, 60
Grimm, Reinhold, 111, 112
Grosz, Georg, 98
Guder, G., 40

Happold, F. C., 137
Heselhaus, Clemens, 8, 9, 45, 57, 112, 120–1
Hille, Peter, 1, 2, 25, 34, 62, 76, 145
Höltgen, K. J., 7, 9, 73, 122–3
Hough, Graham, 5
Hoy, Senna (Johannes Holzman), 88–9, 91, 92
Hyman, S. E., 4

intensification, 38

Jerusalem, 34–5, 64, 67, 149–51
Jewish mysticism, 129–37
Jewish tradition, 8, 123
Judaism, 118–22, 129, 142, 145, 147
Jung, C. G., 7

Katinka, Rachel, 32, 107
Kern, Elga, 16n, 22
Kierkegaard, S., 54
Kissing, Jeanette (mother of E. L.-S.), 19–21, 33, 64ff, 85–6, 95, 97
Kopp, Johanna (grandmother of E. L.-S.), 19
Kraft, Werner, 1, 10, 12, 29, 61, 144
Kraus, Karl, 10, 15, 24, 29–31, 32, 44, 45, 68, 85, 111, 130, 134, 136
Kupper, Margarete, 6–7, 11, 14n

159

INDEX